HELL IN A HANDBASKET

DISPATCHES FROM THE COUNTRY FORMERLY KNOWN AS AMERICA

JEREMY P. TARCHER/PENGUIN
A MEMBER OF PENGUIN GROUP (USA) INC.

For Beverly and Nicholas, always

JEREMY P. TARCHER/PENGUIN
Published by the Penguin Group
Penguin Group (USA) Inc., 375 Hudson Street, New York, New York 10014, USA • Penguin Group (Canada), 90 Eglinton Avenue East, Suite 700, Toronto, Ontario M4P 2Y3, Canada (a division of Pearson Penguin Canada Inc.) • Penguin Books Ltd, 80 Strand, London WC2R 0RL, England • Penguin Ireland, 25 St Stephen's Green, Dublin 2, Ireland (a division of Penguin Books Ltd) • Penguin Group (Australia), 250 Camberwell Road, Camberwell, Victoria 3124, Australia (a division of Pearson Australia Group Pty Ltd) • Penguin Books India Pvt Ltd, 11 Community Centre, Panchsheel Park, New Delhi–110 017, India • Penguin Group (NZ), Cnr Airborne and Rosedale Roads, Albany, Auckland 1310, New Zealand (a division of Pearson New Zealand Ltd) • Penguin Books (South Africa) (Pty) Ltd, 24 Sturdee Avenue, Rosebank, Johannesburg 2196, South Africa

Penguin Books Ltd, Registered Offices: 80 Strand, London WC2R 0RL, England

Library of Congress Cataloging-in-Publication Data

Tomorrow, Tom, date.
Hell in a handbasket : dispatches from the country formerly known as America / Tom Tomorrow.
p.   cm.
ISBN 1-58542-458-7
1. United States—Politics and government—2001– —Caricatures and cartoons.   2. Bush, George W. (George Walker), 1946 —Caricatures and cartoons.   3. Politicians—United States—Caricatures and cartoons. 4. Political culture—United States—Caricatures and cartoons.   I. Title.
E902.T66   2006   2005052896
973.931'092—dc22

Printed in China
1   3   5   7   9   10   8   6   4   2

This book is printed on acid-free paper. ⊗

BOOK DESIGN BY MEIGHAN CAVANAUGH

COVER DESIGN BY TOM TOMORROW

Most Tarcher/Penguin books are available at special quantity discounts for bulk purchase for sales promotions, premiums, fund-raising, and educational needs. Special books or book excerpts also can be created to fit specific needs. For details, write Penguin Group (USA) Inc. Special Markets, 375 Hudson Street, New York, NY 10014.

While the author has made every effort to provide accurate Internet addresses at the time of publication, neither the publisher nor the author assumes any responsibility for errors, or for changes that occur after publication. Further, the publisher does not have any control over and does not assume any responsibility for author or third-party websites or their content.

THIS MODERN WORLD

by TOM TOMORROW

THE BUSH ADMINISTRATION GUIDE TO ACHIEVING CONSENSUS

BROACH THE TOPIC GRADUALLY.

--AND THAT IS WHY I AM PROUD TO SALUTE MOTHERHOOD *AND* APPLE PIE!

AND BY THE WAY, I'M GONNA INVADE IRAQ.

GOD BLESS YOU ALL AND GOD BLESS AMERICA!

LET THE PUNDITS MAKE YOUR CASE FOR YOU--SUCH AS IT IS.

SADDAM ONCE USED WEAPONS OF MASS DESTRUCTION ON HIS OWN PEOPLE, YOU KNOW!

MY *GOD*--THE PRESIDENT HAS TO *DO* SOMETHING!

WHEN REPORTERS ASK QUESTIONS, ACT AS IF YOU'VE NEVER REALLY GIVEN THE MATTER MUCH THOUGHT.

SIR, HOW SOON DO YOU INTEND TO INVADE IRAQ?

I HAVE ABSOLUTELY NO *IDEA* WHAT YOU'RE TALKING ABOUT! THIS MUST BE ANOTHER ONE OF YOUR CRAZY *MEDIA FEEDING FRENZIES!*

IGNORE CONGRESS UNTIL THEY *BEG* FOR THE RIGHT TO RUBBER STAMP YOUR PLANS.

HE *CANNOT* GO TO WAR WITHOUT OUR AUTHORIZATION--

--WHICH OF *COURSE* WE'LL GIVE HIM! WE JUST WANT TO BE *ASKED!*

BEFORE YOU KNOW IT, THE WHOLE WHOLE THING WILL SEEM PRETTY MUCH *INEVITABLE*--

DOESN'T BRENT SCOWCROFT REALIZE THAT WE HAVE NO *CHOICE* BUT TO INVADE IRAQ?

WHAT PLANET IS THAT TREE-HUGGING PEACENIK WACKO *FROM*, ANYWAY?

--AND THEN YOU'RE HOME FREE.

THE AMERICAN PEOPLE *CLEARLY* BELIEVE SADDAM IS A THREAT!

WE ARE BUT THEIR HUMBLE SERVANTS!

BOMBS AWAY!

TOM TOMORROW©2002

1

THIS MODERN WORLD

by TOM TOMORROW

OCTOBER, 2002: FEARING A VOTER BACKLASH, DEMOCRATS VOTE TO GIVE BUSH AUTHORITY TO ATTACK IRAQ.

THE COUNTRY NEEDS TO, UM, SPEAK WITH ONE VOICE. FOR THE MOMENT.

BUT ONCE WE GET PAST THE MIDTERM ELECTIONS, BOY, THOSE REPUBLICANS BETTER **WATCH OUT!**

DECEMBER, 2002: THE MIDTERM ELECTIONS ARE OVER, BUT DEMOCRATS CONTINUE TO BIDE THEIR TIME.

WELL, YOU KNOW, THE PRESIDENT'S APPROVAL RATINGS ARE STILL REASONABLY STRONG RIGHT NOW!

BUT THE MOMENT HIS NUMBERS DROP, WE'LL **DEFINITELY** SPRING INTO ACTION!

NOVEMBER, 2004: DECIDING THAT THEY WILL PROBABLY LOSE THE PRESIDENTIAL ELECTIONS, DEMOCRATS DECLINE TO NOMINATE A CANDIDATE. GEORGE W. BUSH WINS A SECOND TERM BY DEFAULT.

WE JUST DIDN'T WANT TO WEAKEN OUR CHANCES FOR 2008!

BUT AS SOON AS **I'M** IN THE OVAL OFFICE, WE'LL START KICKING SOME REPUBLICAN BUTT FOR **REAL!**

JUNE, 2006: THE PRESIDENT STRIPS CONGRESS OF ALL BUT CEREMONIAL DUTIES. THE DEMOCRATIC RESPONSE IS SUBDUED.

WE DON'T FEEL IT WOULD BE APPROPRIATE TO OPPOSE THE PRESIDENT RIGHT NOW, WHAT WITH THE VARIOUS WARS AND ALL.

BUT ONE OF THESE DAYS, THE SPARKS ARE REALLY GONNA FLY--BELIEVE YOU **ME!**

AUGUST, 2010: PRESIDENT-FOR-LIFE BUSH DECLARES MARTIAL LAW AND DISBANDS THE LEGISLATIVE AND JUDICIAL BRANCHES COMPLETELY. DEMOCRATS VOICE NO OBJECTION.

WE DON'T WANT ANYONE TO THINK WE'RE **SOFT ON TERROR!**

BUT IF THE STATE OF EMERGENCY IS EVER LIFTED-- **THEN** WE'LL STAND UP TO THE ADMINISTRATION FOR **SURE!**

JANUARY, 2143: THE CRYOGENICALLY PRESERVED BRAINS OF TOM DASCHLE AND HILLARY CLINTON CONSIDER ISSUING A STATEMENT SUPPORTING THE RESTORATION OF DEMOCRACY.

NOT RIGHT **AWAY**, OF COURSE-- BUT MAYBE IN ANOTHER TWENTY OR THIRTY YEARS...DEPENDING ON WHAT THE OPINION POLLS SAY...

AND **THAT'S** WHEN WE'LL START TO SEE SOME **REAL** CHANGE AROUND HERE!

TOM TOMORROW©10-23-02

THIS MODERN WORLD

by TOM TOMORROW

THE ARGUMENT GOES SOMETHING LIKE THIS: SURE, THE U.S. BACKED SADDAM FOR DECADES--AND, BY SOME ACCOUNTS, EVEN AIDED HIS RISE TO POWER--BUT THAT ONLY *INCREASES* OUR MORAL OBLIGATION TO BOMB THE HELL OUT OF IRAQ *NOW*.

SO THE HORRIBLY MISGUIDED POLICIES OF THE PAST ACTUALLY *JUSTIFY* THE HORRIBLY MISGUIDED POLICIES OF THE *PRESENT*?

EXACTLY! THE PRESIDENT HAS A *DUTY* TO, UM, DO EXACTLY WHAT HE WANTED TO DO ANYWAY!

AND WE'LL *CERTAINLY* GET IT RIGHT *THIS* TIME!

IT'S A CLEVER RHETORICAL STRATEGY--AND ONE WHICH *DICK CHENEY* MIGHT FIND USEFUL, IF HE'S EVER FORCED TO RELEASE THOSE ENERGY TASK FORCE RECORDS...

--AND YOU ADMIT THAT YOU WERE *PERSONALLY RE-SPONSIBLE* FOR CALIFORNIA'S FAKE ENERGY CRISIS?

YES--WHICH IS WHY IT IS NOW MY *MORAL DUTY* TO *REMAIN IN OFFICE* AND CONVENE *ANOTHER* ENERGY TASK FORCE!

WELL--ALL RIGHT, THEN!

THE SUPREME COURT'S *FLORIDA FIVE* COULD PROB-ABLY BENEFIT FROM THIS ONE AS WELL...

SURE, WE SUBVERTED THE CONSTITUTION TO INSTALL OUR BOY *GEORGE* IN OFFICE...

...BUT THAT JUST MEANS THAT WE HAVE AN EVEN *GREATER* RESPON-SIBILITY TO OVERSEE THE *NEXT* PRESIDENTIAL ELECTION!

HEH, HEH.

...NOT TO MENTION ANYONE *ELSE* WITH AN AWKWARD INDISCRETION IN THEIR PAST...

SORRY ABOUT THE CROSS-COUNTRY KILLING SPREE, YOUR HONOR--BUT THE WAY *I* SEE IT, I HAVE A *MORAL OBLIGATION* TO WALK OUT OF THIS COURTROOM A *FREE MAN*.

HOW ELSE CAN I *POS-SIBLY* EVER ATONE FOR MY CRIMES?

WELL, SINCE YOU PUT IT THAT WAY--*CASE DISMISSED!*

TOM TOMORROW©10-30-02

3

THIS MODERN WORLD

by TOM TOMORROW

PART ONE: IN WHICH THE CARTOONIST INDULGES IN A SMALL FLIGHT OF FANCY

TO HONOR THE MEMORY OF PAUL WELLSTONE, I HAVE DECIDED TO CAMPAIGN RELENTLESSLY AGAINST THE ADMINISTRATION'S WAR ON IRAQ-- NO MATTER **WHAT** THE POLITICAL CONSEQUENCES MAY BE!

I WON'T REST UNTIL PAUL'S DREAM OF **UNIVERSAL HEALTH COVERAGE** HAS BEEN REALIZED-- AND I DON'T GIVE A **DAMN** WHAT MY BACKERS IN THE INSURANCE INDUSTRY THINK ABOUT IT!

WE MUST ALSO FIGHT FOR A **LIVING WAGE** FOR THE WORKING POOR!

AND WORK TO UNDO THE DAMAGE OF **WELFARE REFORM**!

AND ENACT **REAL** CAMPAIGN FINANCE REFORM!

AND--

AND--

AND--

PART TWO: IN WHICH HE RETURNS TO REALITY

MAYBE IF WE GIVE GEORGE BUSH EVERYTHING HE WANTS FOR THE REST OF HIS TERM, THE VOTERS WILL LIKE US BETTER.

AND THEN WE **MIGHT** BE ABLE TO HANG ON TO OUR JOBS A LITTLE LONGER!

IT'S WHAT PAUL WOULD HAVE **WANTED** US TO DO.

TOM TOMORROW © 11-7-02

4

THIS MODERN WORLD

by TOM TOMORROW

FROM SEA TO SHINING SEA, AMERICANS ARE PONDERING...*WORST CASE SCENARIOS!*

WHAT IF SADDAM HAS A DIABOLICAL PLAN TO REPLACE THE LEADERS OF THE FREE WORLD WITH IDENTICAL *CLONES* WHOSE ONLY ALLEGIANCE IS TO *HIM?*

THE CONSEQUENCES COULD BE *DIRE!*

OR MAYBE HE'S TRYING TO DEVELOP A *TIME MACHINE* SO HE CAN TRAVEL BACK TO 1776 AND PREVENT THE UNITED STATES FROM EVER *EXISTING!*

THE THREAT HE POSES CANNOT BE UNDER-ESTIMATED!

HE *COULD* BE IN CONTACT WITH A RACE OF *KILLER ALIEN ROBOTS* WHO WANT TO ENSLAVE OUR PLANET AND INSTALL *HIM* AS HUMANITY'S *SUPREME OVERLORD!*

IT IS TRULY TERRIFYING TO CONTEMPLATE!

AHEM!

UM--HERE'S A SCENARIO FOR YOU: WHAT IF THE INVASION OF IRAQ TURNS OUT TO BE A COMPLETE *CATASTROPHE*--COSTING THOUSANDS OF LIVES, SETTING OFF OTHER WARS IN THE REGION, AND ULTIMATELY DOING *FAR* MORE HARM THAN GOOD?

YEAH, RIGHT.

SNICKER!

*ANY*WAY--

--WHAT IF HE'S TRAINING AN ARMY OF GIANT *MUTANT LIZARDS* WHO CAN SHOOT DEADLY *LASER BEAMS* OUT OF THEIR *EYEBALLS?*

WE'D BETTER ATTACK SOON--JUST TO BE *SAFE!*

SIGH... I DON'T KNOW WHY I BOTHER...

TOM TOMORROW©2002

5

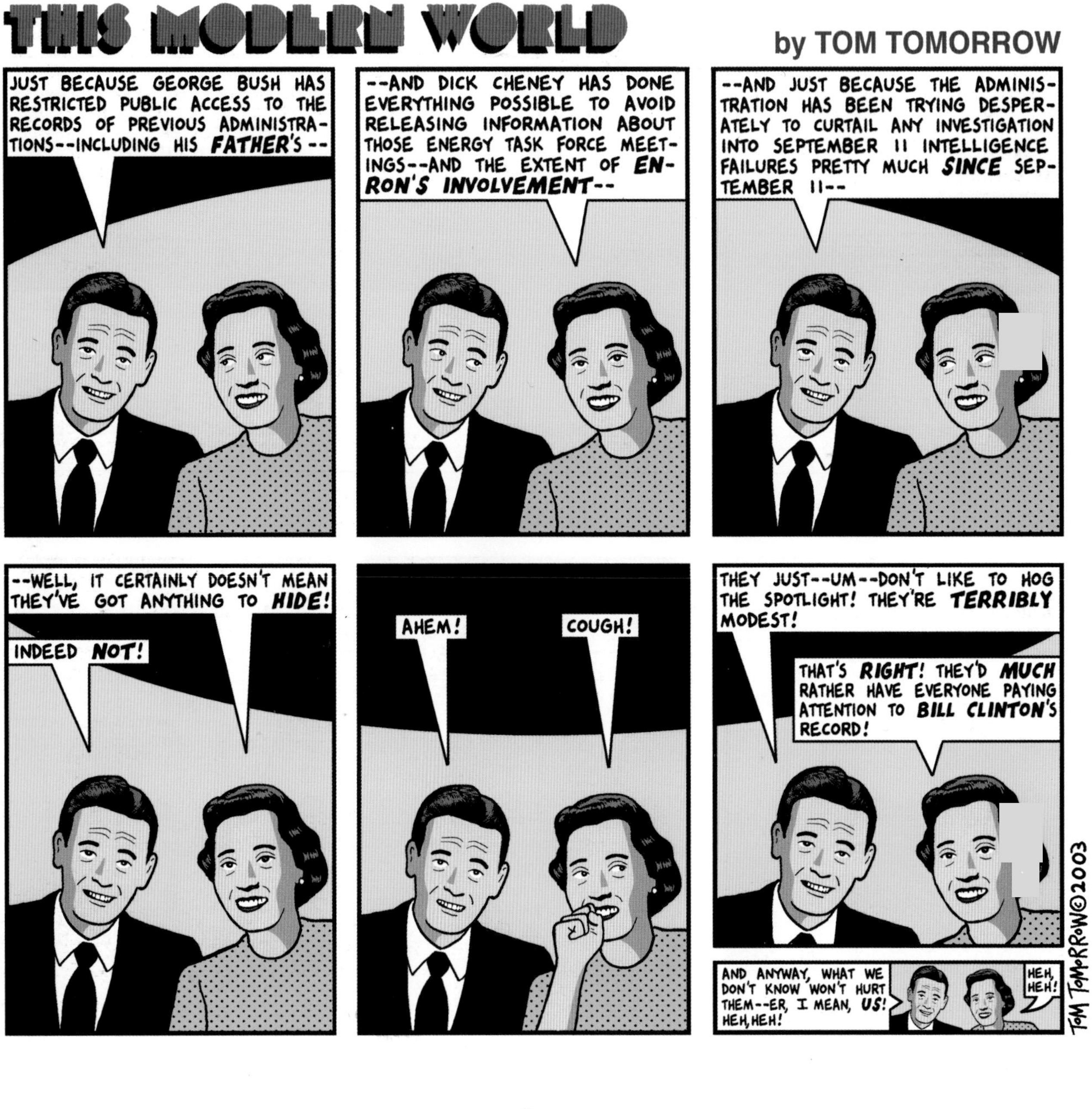
THIS MODERN WORLD
by TOM TOMORROW
JUST BECAUSE GEORGE BUSH HAS RESTRICTED PUBLIC ACCESS TO THE RECORDS OF PREVIOUS ADMINISTRATIONS--INCLUDING HIS FATHER'S--
--AND DICK CHENEY HAS DONE EVERYTHING POSSIBLE TO AVOID RELEASING INFORMATION ABOUT THOSE ENERGY TASK FORCE MEETINGS--AND THE EXTENT OF ENRON'S INVOLVEMENT--
--AND JUST BECAUSE THE ADMINISTRATION HAS BEEN TRYING DESPERATELY TO CURTAIL ANY INVESTIGATION INTO SEPTEMBER 11 INTELLIGENCE FAILURES PRETTY MUCH SINCE SEPTEMBER 11--
--WELL, IT CERTAINLY DOESN'T MEAN THEY'VE GOT ANYTHING TO HIDE!
INDEED NOT!
AHEM!
COUGH!
THEY JUST--UM--DON'T LIKE TO HOG THE SPOTLIGHT! THEY'RE TERRIBLY MODEST!
THAT'S RIGHT! THEY'D MUCH RATHER HAVE EVERYONE PAYING ATTENTION TO BILL CLINTON'S RECORD!
AND ANYWAY, WHAT WE DON'T KNOW WON'T HURT THEM--ER, I MEAN, US! HEH, HEH!
HEH, HEH!
TOM TOMORROW©2003

THIS MODERN WORLD

by TOM TOMORROW

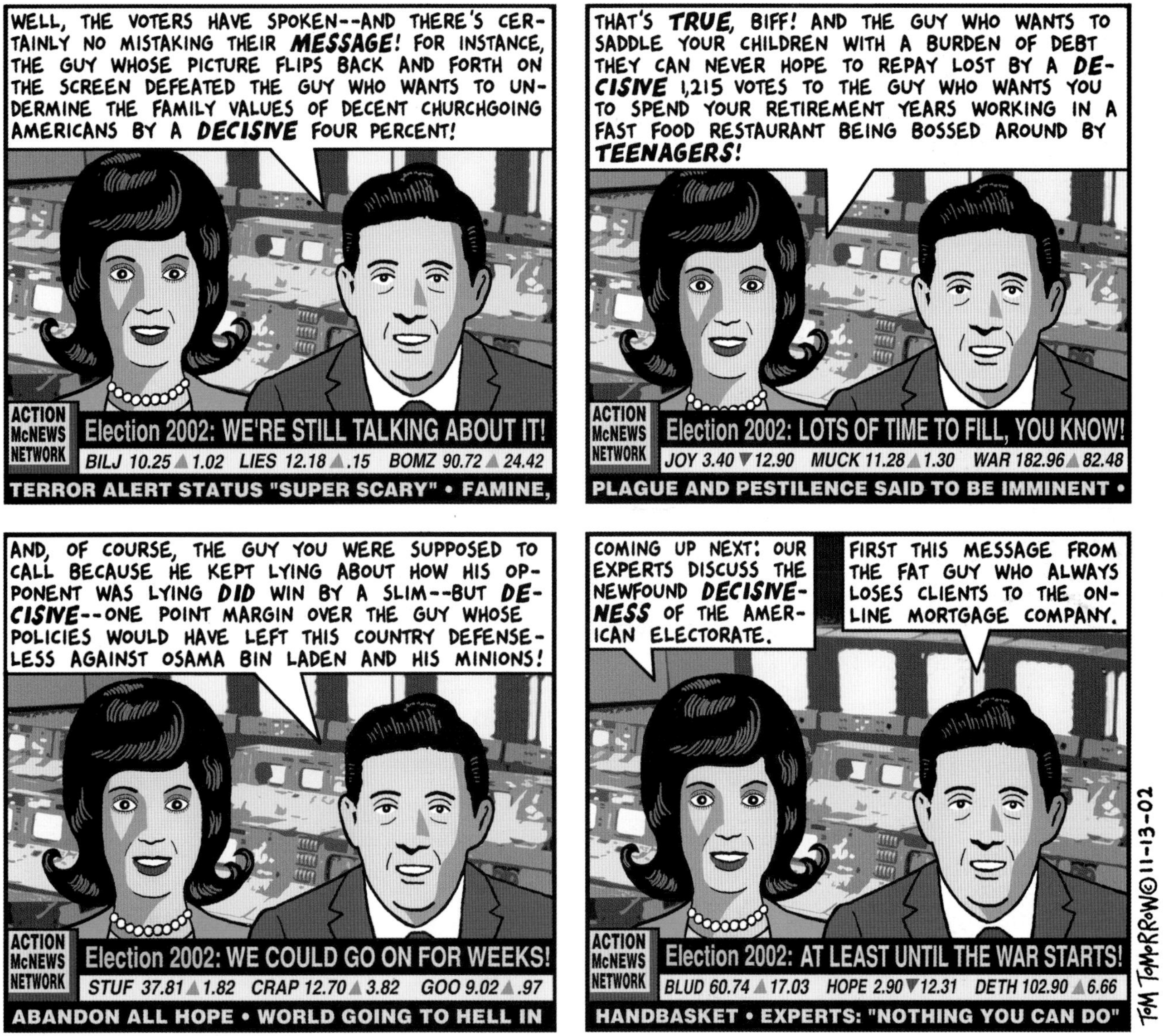
WELL, THE VOTERS HAVE SPOKEN--AND THERE'S CERTAINLY NO MISTAKING THEIR MESSAGE! FOR INSTANCE, THE GUY WHOSE PICTURE FLIPS BACK AND FORTH ON THE SCREEN DEFEATED THE GUY WHO WANTS TO UNDERMINE THE FAMILY VALUES OF DECENT CHURCHGOING AMERICANS BY A DECISIVE FOUR PERCENT!
ACTION McNEWS NETWORK
Election 2002: WE'RE STILL TALKING ABOUT IT!
BILJ 10.25 ▲1.02 LIES 12.18 ▲.15 BOMZ 90.72 ▲24.42
TERROR ALERT STATUS "SUPER SCARY" • FAMINE,
THAT'S TRUE, BIFF! AND THE GUY WHO WANTS TO SADDLE YOUR CHILDREN WITH A BURDEN OF DEBT THEY CAN NEVER HOPE TO REPAY LOST BY A DECISIVE 1,215 VOTES TO THE GUY WHO WANTS YOU TO SPEND YOUR RETIREMENT YEARS WORKING IN A FAST FOOD RESTAURANT BEING BOSSED AROUND BY TEENAGERS!
ACTION McNEWS NETWORK
Election 2002: LOTS OF TIME TO FILL, YOU KNOW!
JOY 3.40 ▼12.90 MUCK 11.28 ▲1.30 WAR 182.96 ▲82.48
PLAGUE AND PESTILENCE SAID TO BE IMMINENT •
AND, OF COURSE, THE GUY YOU WERE SUPPOSED TO CALL BECAUSE HE KEPT LYING ABOUT HOW HIS OPPONENT WAS LYING DID WIN BY A SLIM--BUT DECISIVE--ONE POINT MARGIN OVER THE GUY WHOSE POLICIES WOULD HAVE LEFT THIS COUNTRY DEFENSELESS AGAINST OSAMA BIN LADEN AND HIS MINIONS!
ACTION McNEWS NETWORK
Election 2002: WE COULD GO ON FOR WEEKS!
STUF 37.81 ▲1.82 CRAP 12.70 ▲3.82 GOO 9.02 ▲.97
ABANDON ALL HOPE • WORLD GOING TO HELL IN
COMING UP NEXT: OUR EXPERTS DISCUSS THE NEWFOUND DECISIVENESS OF THE AMERICAN ELECTORATE.
FIRST THIS MESSAGE FROM THE FAT GUY WHO ALWAYS LOSES CLIENTS TO THE ONLINE MORTGAGE COMPANY.
ACTION McNEWS NETWORK
Election 2002: AT LEAST UNTIL THE WAR STARTS!
BLUD 60.74 ▲17.03 HOPE 2.90 ▼12.31 DETH 102.90 ▲6.66
HANDBASKET • EXPERTS: "NOTHING YOU CAN DO"
TOM TOMORROW © 11-13-02

THIS MODERN WORLD

by TOM TOMORROW

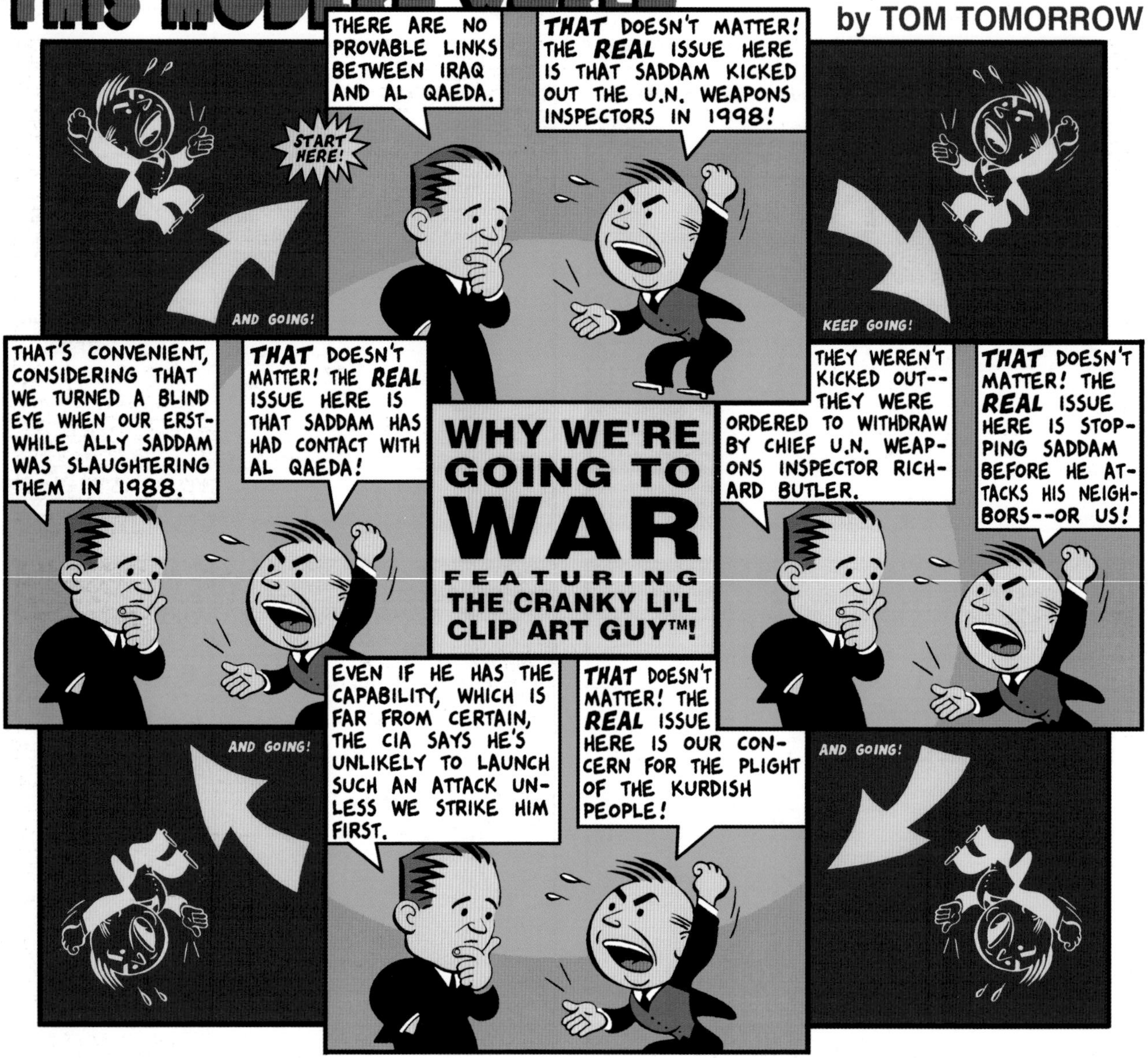
WHY WE'RE GOING TO WAR
FEATURING THE CRANKY LI'L CLIP ART GUY™!
START HERE!
THERE ARE NO PROVABLE LINKS BETWEEN IRAQ AND AL QAEDA.
THAT DOESN'T MATTER! THE REAL ISSUE HERE IS THAT SADDAM KICKED OUT THE U.N. WEAPONS INSPECTORS IN 1998!
KEEP GOING!
THEY WEREN'T KICKED OUT-- THEY WERE ORDERED TO WITHDRAW BY CHIEF U.N. WEAPONS INSPECTOR RICHARD BUTLER.
THAT DOESN'T MATTER! THE REAL ISSUE HERE IS STOPPING SADDAM BEFORE HE ATTACKS HIS NEIGHBORS--OR US!
AND GOING!
EVEN IF HE HAS THE CAPABILITY, WHICH IS FAR FROM CERTAIN, THE CIA SAYS HE'S UNLIKELY TO LAUNCH SUCH AN ATTACK UNLESS WE STRIKE HIM FIRST.
THAT DOESN'T MATTER! THE REAL ISSUE HERE IS OUR CONCERN FOR THE PLIGHT OF THE KURDISH PEOPLE!
AND GOING!
THAT'S CONVENIENT, CONSIDERING THAT WE TURNED A BLIND EYE WHEN OUR ERSTWHILE ALLY SADDAM WAS SLAUGHTERING THEM IN 1988.
THAT DOESN'T MATTER! THE REAL ISSUE HERE IS THAT SADDAM HAS HAD CONTACT WITH AL QAEDA!
AND GOING!

THIS MODERN WORLD

by TOM TOMORROW

THIS WEEK: A RAINY DAY "WAR ON TERROR" FUN GAME!

CAN *YOU* TELL WHICH OF THE FOLLOWING PANELS DESCRIBE ACTUAL EVENTS--AND WHICH ARE SIMPLY *OUTLANDISH SATIRE?*

WHY--THIS COULD PROVIDE LITERALLY *MINUTES* OF AMUSEMENT!

LET'S GET *STARTED!*

1) DID REPUBLICANS *REALLY* INSERT A LAST-MINUTE PROVISION IN THE HOMELAND SECURITY BILL DESIGNED TO PROTECT *ELI LILLY* FROM LAWSUITS OVER A VACCINE PRESERVATIVE ANECDOTALLY LINKED TO *AUTISM?*

PERHAPS THEY WERE AFRAID THAT THE PARENTS OF AUTISTIC CHILDREN MIGHT DONATE ANY MONEY THEY WERE AWARDED TO *AL QAEDA!*

YOU CAN'T BE TOO CAREFUL *THESE* DAYS!

2) DID THE U.S. ARMY *REALLY* EXPEL SIX HIGHLY-TRAINED ARABIC TRANSLATORS...AFTER FINDING OUT THAT THEY ARE *GAY?*

ADMITTEDLY, WE'VE GOT A DRASTIC SHORTAGE OF ARABIC SPEAKERS RIGHT NOW--

--BUT HEY--WE'VE STILL GOT TO KEEP OUR PRIORITIES *STRAIGHT!*

SO TO SPEAK.

3) AND DID THE ADMINISTRATION *REALLY* PROPOSE THE CREATION OF AN "INFORMATION AWARENESS OFFICE" TO MONITOR EVERY CITIZEN'S EMAIL, CREDIT CARD TRANSACTIONS, TRAVEL, AND MORE--TO BE OVERSEEN BY IRAN-CONTRA CONSPIRATOR *JOHN POINDEXTER?*

SURE, HE ILLEGALLY FUNDED A SECRET WAR IN NICARAGUA WITH ARMS SALES TO *IRAN*--AND THEN LIED TO *CONGRESS* ABOUT IT--

--BUT I'M *SURE* WE CAN TRUST HIM *NOW!*

NICE LOGO.

ANSWER: THEY'RE ALL TRUE. FEEL ANY SAFER?

TOM TOMORROW © 2002

THIS MODERN WORLD

by TOM TOMORROW

WHEN YOUNG BILLY THOMPSON FAILED HIS EIGHTH GRADE CIVICS CLASS, HIS TEACHER TRIED TO WARN HIM OF THE CONSEQUENCES.

DON'T YOU UNDERSTAND, YOUNG MAN? THIS GRADE IS GOING TO GO ON YOUR *PERMANENT RECORD!!*

WHATEVER.

1. Executive
2. Legislative
3. Judicial

HIS TRANSCRIPT WAS PROMPTLY TRANSMITTED TO THE NEW *INFORMATION AWARENESS OFFICE,* WHERE IT WAS FILED AWAY IN THEIR MASSIVE DATA-BASE OF *EVERY AMERICAN CITIZEN...*

HMMM--FAILED *CIVICS,* EH? WE'D BETTER KEEP AN EYE ON THIS ONE.

HE *COULD* TURN OUT TO BE A *TROUBLEMAKER.*

SEVERAL YEARS PASSED...AND THEN ONE DAY, BILLY-- NOW A YOUNG ADULT--PURCHASED A POTENTIALLY SUBVERSIVE BOOK FROM AN ONLINE RETAILER.

CODE RED! WILLIAM THOMPSON JUST BOUGHT A COPY OF *CATCHER IN THE RYE!*

WILLIAM THOMPSON? ISN'T HE THE ONE WHO FAILED EIGHTH GRADE *CIVICS?*

AND THEN BILLY THOMPSON BELATEDLY LEARNED AN IMPORTANT LESSON: WHEN TEACHERS WARN YOU ABOUT YOUR PERMANENT RECORD THESE DAYS--THEY *REALLY MEAN IT...*

MR. THOMPSON? WE HAVE REASON TO BELIEVE THAT YOU'VE BEEN AN AMERICA-HATING MAL-CONTENT SINCE AT LEAST THE *EIGHTH GRADE,* WHEN YOU COULDN'T EVEN BE BOTHERED TO LEARN THE FUNDAMENTALS OF OUR DEMOCRACY!

COME WITH US, PLEASE.

BUT--BUT--

TOM TOMORROW©12-04-02

THIS MODERN WORLD

by TOM TOMORROW

LANGUAGE IS STILL A VIRUS

ANOTHER LOOK AT HOW IDIOTIC IDEAS ENTER THE POLITICAL MAINSTREAM

A FEW WEEKS AGO, A TRIAL BALLOON WAS FLOATED ON THE EDITORIAL PAGE OF THE WALL STREET JOURNAL.

IT SAYS HERE THAT THE POOR ARE "LUCKY DUCKIES" WHO ARE *INSUFFICIENTLY TAXED!*

I'LL BET THEY DO NOT EVEN *REALIZE* HOW FORTUNATE THEY ARE!

HOW I *ENVY* THEM!

THE WALL STREET JOURNAL

What's News

THEY'RE CLEARLY HOPING THAT THE IDEA WILL CATCH ON--THAT TALK RADIO HOSTS, FOX NEWS ANCHORS, AND OTHER CONSERVATIVE OPINION-SHAPERS WILL PICK UP THE BALL AND *RUN* WITH IT.

THERE'S AN ENTIRE CLASS OF PEOPLE IN THIS COUNTRY WHO PAY *NO TAXES WHATSOEVER!* I ASK YOU--IS THAT *FAIR?*

WHY--IT CERTAINLY IS NOT!

THEY'RE PROBABLY LIVING A LIFE OF STATE-SUBSIDIZED LEISURE, EVEN AS WE SPEAK!

IF THIS HAPPENS, AN IDEA THAT SOUNDS LIKE SWIFTIAN *SATIRE* WILL PROBABLY--THROUGH SHEER FORCE OF REPETITION--SOON BECOME *CONVENTIONAL WISDOM*--

THOSE MINIMUM WAGE TAX SLACKERS ARE BLEEDING WEALTHY AMERICANS *DRY!*

IT IS AN OUTRAGE! WHAT DO THEY THINK THIS *IS*-- COMMUNIST *CHINA?*

BUS STOP

--WHICH WILL, IN TURN, BE USED TO JUSTIFY THE UNDERLYING *GOAL*--THE IMPLEMENTATION OF SOME SORT OF APPALLINGLY REGRESSIVE TAX *"REFORM"*...

YES, THAT'S RIGHT--WE *DO* WANT TO SHIFT THE TAX BURDEN ONTO THE BACKS OF LOW-INCOME AMERICANS.

EVERYONE *KNOWS* IT'S THE ONLY *FAIR* THING TO *DO!*

HAVEN'T YOU BEEN WATCHING *FOX NEWS?*

...AND THE COUNTRY'S JOURNEY TO HELL IN A HANDBASKET WILL CONTINUE UNIMPEDED.

TOM TOMORROW© 12-11-02

THIS MODERN WORLD

by TOM TOMORROW

IT'S TIME ONCE AGAIN FOR THE AD-VENTURES OF **DONKEY-MAN** AND **HILLARY, THE SENATORIAL WONDER!**

DONKEY-MAN--MYSTERIOUS EXPLOSIONS HAVE BEEN EMANATING FROM THE GROUNDS OF THE VICE-PRESIDENT'S RESIDENCE FOR **MONTHS!*** WE'VE GOT TO **DO SOMETHING!**

YOU'RE **RIGHT!** I'LL CON-VENE A **FOCUS GROUP!**

*THIS IS TRUE.

MEANWHILE, IN A **SECRET LAIR** BENEATH DICK CHENEY'S HOME

BOSS, THE NOISE FROM THE TIME MACHINE'S **TEMPORAL RE-ENTRY SEQUENCE** IS BEGIN-NING TO AROUSE **SUS-PICION!**

LET THE FOOLS **WON-DER,** KARL! THEY'LL **NEVER** GUESS THE **TRUTH!**

BWAH HA HA HA!

I'M BACK FROM THE **PAST,** MR. CHENEY--WITH OUR **NEWEST RECRUIT!**

TIME CHINE

?

WHERE-- WHERE **AM I?**

IT'S THE YEAR 2002, ADMIRAL POINDEXTER-- AND WE NEED YOU TO HEAD A SECRETIVE IN-FORMATION-GATHERING BUREAUCRACY DESIGNED TO SPY ON **AMERICAN CITIZENS!**

I CAN DO THAT.

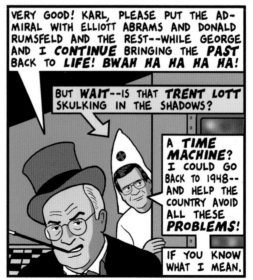

VERY GOOD! KARL, PLEASE PUT THE AD-MIRAL WITH ELLIOTT ABRAMS AND DONALD RUMSFELD AND THE REST--WHILE GEORGE AND I **CONTINUE** BRINGING THE **PAST** BACK TO **LIFE!** BWAH HA HA HA HA!

BUT **WAIT**--IS THAT **TRENT LOTT** SKULKING IN THE SHADOWS?

A **TIME MACHINE?** I COULD GO BACK TO 1948-- AND HELP THE COUNTRY AVOID ALL THESE **PROBLEMS!**

IF YOU KNOW WHAT I MEAN.

AND **WHERE** IS THE **DEMOCRATIC DU(**

SHOULDN'T WE, UM, GET **GOING,** DONKEY-MAN?

AS SOON AS I ANALYZE THIS **POLLING DATA!**

WHAT HAPPENS **NEXT?** STAY **TUNED!**

TOM TOMORROW ©12-18-02

Panel 1: SPARKY, THE MODERN REPUBLICAN PARTY HAS **NO PLACE** FOR A NEANDERTHAL LIKE TRENT LOTT.

THAT'S NICE--BUT DON'T PULL A MUSCLE PATTING YOURSELF ON THE BACK.

Panel 2: I MEAN, IT'S NOT AS IF LOTT'S VIEWS SHOULD HAVE COME AS A **SURPRISE** TO YOU--THIS **IS** THE GUY WHO'S BEEN INVOLVED WITH THE WHITE SUPREMACIST **COUNCIL OF CONSERVATIVE CITIZENS** FOR **YEARS**--

Panel 3: --AND WHO EVEN WENT SO FAR AS TO PRAISE THE GROUP FOR HAVING "THE **RIGHT PRINCIPLES** AND THE **RIGHT PHILOSOPHY!**"

AND IT'S NOT AS IF LOTT IS EXACTLY AN **ABERRATION** HERE...

Panel 4: WHAT ABOUT **DON NICKLES**, WHO, ALONG WITH LOTT, TRIED TO BLOCK THE AMBASSADORSHIP OF JAMES HORMEL--SOLELY BECAUSE HORMEL WAS **GAY?**

AND OF COURSE, THERE'S **JOHN ASHCROFT**--

Panel 5: --WHO ONCE THANKED THE NEO-CONFEDERATE **SOUTHERN PARTISAN** MAGAZINE--WHICH SOLD T-SHIRTS CELEBRATING THE ASSASSINATION OF **ABRAHAM LINCOLN**--FOR HELPING TO "SET THE RECORD **STRAIGHT!**"

I DON'T HEAR ANY OF YOU MODERATE REPUBLICANS DENOUNCING EITHER OF **THEM!**

Panel 6: WELL, YOU CAN REST ASSURED WE **WILL**--

--IF THEY EVER CREATE AN EMBARRASSING PUBLIC FUROR WHICH THREATENS TO UNDERMINE THE REPUBLICAN PARTY'S CAREFULLY-CONSTRUCTED FACADE OF TOLERANCE AND DIVERSITY, THAT IS!

YOUR STEADFAST DEVOTION TO PRINCIPLE IS TRULY INSPIRING TO BEHOLD.

TOM TOMORROW©2002

THIS MODERN WORLD

by TOM TOMORROW

REMEMBER THAT CONVERSATION PAT ROBERTSON HAD WITH JERRY FALWELL ON "THE 700 CLUB" A FEW DAYS AFTER THE SEPTEMBER 11 ATTACKS?

I REALLY BELIEVE THAT THE PAGANS AND THE ABORTIONISTS AND THE FEMINISTS AND THE GAYS AND THE LESBIANS...ALL OF THEM WHO HAVE TRIED TO SECULARIZE AMERICA--I POINT THE FINGER IN THEIR FACE AND SAY, "*YOU* HELPED THIS HAPPEN!"*

I TOTALLY CONCUR!

*ACTUAL QUOTES, OF COURSE. BUT YOU KNEW THAT.

WELL, ROBERTSON WAS (AND STILL °IS, AS FAR AS WE KNOW) HEAVILY INVESTED IN A GOLD MINING OPERATION IN *LIBERIA*--IN PARTNERSHIP WITH THAT COUNTRY'S BRUTAL DICTATOR, *CHARLES TAYLOR*--

I BELIEVE THAT TORTURE AND SUMMARY EXECUTIONS ARE THE *KEY* TO AN *ORDERLY SOCIETY*!

WHAT'S THAT? YOU SAY YOU CHERISH THE VALUES OF FREEDOM AND DEMOCRACY? WELL, SO DO *I*!

NOW LET'S GET THIS CONTRACT SIGNED, SHALL WE?

--AND HERE'S THE INTERESTING PART: AT ABOUT THE SAME TIME ROBERTSON AND FALWELL WERE BUSY CASTING STONES TOWARD SECULAR HUMANISTS, ROBERTSON'S PAL *TAYLOR* WAS ACTUALLY *PROVIDING SANCTUARY TO AL QAEDA OPERATIVES*, IN RETURN FOR A MILLION DOLLAR PAYOFF. *

YOU HAVE MADE IT POSSIBLE FOR US TO CONTINUE OUR HOLY WAR AGAINST THE PAGANS AND ABORTIONISTS AND HOMOSEXUALS AND ALL THE OTHER NONBELIEVERS, PRESIDENT TAYLOR!

YOU KNOW, YOU REMIND ME OF THIS *OTHER* FELLOW I KNOW...

*"REPORT SAYS AFRICANS HARBORED AL QAEDA," WASHINGTON POST, 12/29/02

YOU PROBABLY SEE WHERE WE'RE GOING WITH THIS.

ER-- WE HAVEN'T REALLY BEEN ABLE TO FIND ANY PROVABLE LINK BETWEEN OSAMA AND SADDAM--

--BUT THERE *IS* A CLEAR CONNECTION BETWEEN AL QAEDA AND THE *CHRISTIAN BROADCASTING NETWORK*!

WELL, THEN, *SEND IN THE TROOPS!* I WANT THIS ROBERTSON CHARACTER IN A CAGE AT CAMP X-RAY BY THE *END OF THE DAY*!

TOM TOMORROW©2003

14

THIS MODERN WORLD

by TOM TOMORROW

THE PRESIDENT MAKES A STARTLING ANNOUNCEMENT!

BECAUSE THE MOON *MAY* SOMEDAY BREAK OUT OF ORBIT AND CRASH INTO THE EARTH--

--I HAVE DECIDED TO USE OUR NOOKYALUR ARSENAL TO DESTROY IT *NOW!*

DONALD RUMSFELD BEGINS A "CHARM OFFENSIVE"!

SIR, WHAT EVIDENCE DO YOU HAVE THAT THE MOON COULD DESTROY OUR PLANET?

I COULD TELL YOU, BUT THEN I'D HAVE TO KILL YOU. HA, HA!

HA, HA!

AVERAGE CITIZENS GROW INCREASINGLY ALARMED!

THE MOON'S COMPLETELY INHOSPITABLE TO HUMAN LIFE, YOU KNOW! WHY, IF WE *LIVED* THERE, WE'D ALL BE *DEAD!*

IT'S LIKE SOME SORT OF HUGE *PSYCHO KILLER* IN THE *SKY!*

SOON, THE DESTRUCTION OF THE MOON SEEMS LIKE THE *ONLY* SENSIBLE OPTION!

THE DAMNED THING COULD COME CRASHING DOWN ON OUR HEADS AT *ANY MOMENT!*

THE SOONER WE'RE RID OF THAT STUPID HUNK OF ROCK, THE HAPPIER *I'LL* BE!

A FEW LIBERALS DO RAISE TIMID OBJECTIONS--

YOU KNOW, THERE'S REALLY NO TELLING WHAT IMPACT THE DESTRUCTION OF THE MOON WILL HAVE ON THE EARTH'S *OCEANS*--

SNICKER! WHATEVER YOU SAY, MISTER SAVE-THE-WHALES!

--BUT OF COURSE, NO ONE CARES WHAT *THEY* THINK.

THEY WHINE AND COMPLAIN ABOUT DESTROYING THE MOON--BUT DO *THEY* HAVE ANY SOLUTIONS?

THEY PROBABLY JUST WANT US ALL TO SIT AROUND AND WAIT FOR THE MOON TO FALL RIGHT ON OUR *HEADS!*

CRAZY MOON-LOVERS!

TOM TOMORROW©2003

THIS MODERN WORLD

by TOM TOMORROW

IT'S TIME FOR ANOTHER EDITION OF "JUST FOLKS"--THE SHOW WHERE WEALTHY CONSERVATIVE PUNDITS DISCUSS THEIR **DEEP AFFINITY** FOR **ORDINARY AMERICANS!**

SALT OF THE EARTH!

GOD BLESS 'EM!

THEY'RE JUST LIKE US--ONLY **LESS** SO!

OUR TOPIC TONIGHT--DO **ORDINARY AMERICANS** SUPPORT THE PRESIDENT'S PLAN FOR AN UPPER INCOME TAX CUT?

OF **COURSE** THEY DO! ORDINARY AMERICANS AREN'T ALL TWISTED UP INSIDE WITH CLASS ENVY, LIKE THESE **LIBERAL ELITISTS!**

THAT'S RIGHT! ORDINARY AMERICANS ARE HAPPY, **SIMPLE** PEOPLE--LEADING HAPPY, SIMPLE **LIVES!** THEY DON'T HAVE **TIME** FOR ALL THIS BITTERNESS AND RESENTMENT!

YES! ORDINARY AMERICANS ARE TOO BUSY GOING TO **BOWLING ALLEYS** AND **MONSTER TRUCK RALLIES** AND--UM--

--WHATEVER ELSE IT IS THEY DO OUT THERE IN FLYOVER COUNTRY...

HOOTENANNIES! DON'T THEY HAVE HOOTENANNIES?

AND **HAY RIDES!**

SO THERE'S **NO DOUBT ABOUT IT**--ORDINARY AMERICANS **DEFINITELY** SUPPORT TAX CUTS FOR THE WEALTHY!

BOY--**NOBODY** UNDERSTANDS ORDINARY AMERICANS LIKE **WE** DO!

I **READ** ABOUT MONSTER TRUCKS ONCE!

COMING UP NEXT: WHY **ARE** LIBERAL ELITISTS SO OUT OF TOUCH WITH ORDINARY AMERICANS, ANYWAY?

THEY'VE PROBABLY NEVER EVEN **HEARD** OF MONSTER TRUCKS!

FIRST THESE MESSAGES!

Tom Tomorrow ©2003

THIS MODERN WORLD

by TOM TOMORROW

SOME PEOPLE THINK IT'S IMPORTANT TO REDUCE OUR DEPENDENCE ON FOREIGN OIL--

YOU SEE, IF WE COULD JUST RAISE FUEL EFFICIENCY STANDARDS *SLIGHTLY*--

YEAH, SURE! AND I SUPPOSE NEXT YOU'LL WANT US ALL TO DRIVE *GRANOLA POWERED CARS* MADE OUT OF *GORETEX* OR SOMETHING!

HA, HA!

--BUT CLEARLY, THEY *JUST DON'T GET IT!* IF WE HAVE TO ADJUST OUR STANDARD OF LIVING IN ANY WAY WHATSOEVER--WELL--HAVEN'T SADDAM AND HIS TERRORIST BUDDIES *ALREADY WON*?

OUR PLAN TO HUMILIATE THE AMERICANS BY FORCING THEM TO DRIVE SMALLER AND MORE FUEL EFFICIENT VEHICLES HAS BEEN A *FAILURE!*

CURSES! WE DID NOT ANTICIPATE THE *DEPTH* OF THEIR *RESOLVE!*

(A DRAMATIZATION)

SO WE'LL WASTE AS MUCH GAS AS WE *WANT*, THANK YOU VERY MUCH! AFTER ALL, ISN'T THE PROFLIGATE CONSUMPTION OF NATURAL RESOURCES OUR GOD-GIVEN BIRTHRIGHT AS *AMERICANS*?

BUT DIDN'T GOD GIVE THE SPECIFIC RESOURCES IN QUESTION TO *OTHER COUNTRIES*?

YES--BUT HE GAVE *US* AN *ENORMOUS MILITARY BUDGET!*

ENOUGH *THEOLOGY*, YOU TWO! LET'S GO FOR AN AIMLESS RIDE IN MY *LINCOLN NAVIGATOR!*

AND HOW BETTER TO SHOW OUR SUPPORT FOR OUR TROOPS--THAN TO *FLAUNT* OUR ADDICTION TO THE SUBSTANCE FOR WHICH THEY'LL SOON BE *DYING*?

CHECK IT OUT, GUYS! WE'VE GOT A *HUMMER*--JUST LIKE *YOU*! AND IT ONLY GETS *EIGHT MILES TO THE GALLON!*

YOUR SACRIFICES WON'T BE IN *VAIN!*

DEPLOYMENT

WAIT--I THOUGHT THIS WASN'T *ABOUT* THE OIL!

I SUPPOSE YOU STILL BELIEVE IN THE EASTER BUNNY, TOO.

TOM TOMORROW © 1-29-03

17

THIS MODERN WORLD

by TOM TOMORROW

I AM **OUTRAGED** BY THE DETERMINATION OF AN UNELECTED PRESIDENT TO DRAG US INTO AN UNNECESSARY WAR! **AND** I AM OUTRAGED BY HIS ASSERTION THAT WE WILL NOT "PASS OUR PROBLEMS ALONG" TO FUTURE GENERATIONS-- WHEN **HE'S** THE ONE PROPOSING A **TRILLION DOLLAR DEFICIT** OVER THE NEXT FIVE YEARS!

I AM OUTRAGED THAT **ENRON** AND THE OTHER CORPORATE SCANDALS HAVE BEEN EFFECTIVELY **SWEPT UNDER THE CARPET!** AND THAT DICK CHENEY **STILL** HASN'T MADE HIS ENERGY TASK FORCE RECORDS PUBLIC! **AND** THAT THE S.E.C. HAS ACTUALLY JUST **WEAKENED** ACCOUNTING INDUSTRY OVERSIGHT!

AND I AM OUTRAGED BY THE ADMINISTRATION'S ATTEMPTS TO UNDERMINE **AFFIRMATIVE ACTION**--NOT TO **MENTION** THEIR STEALTH CAMPAIGN AGAINST ABORTION RIGHTS--AND THE **BILLIONS** THEY'RE POURING INTO AN ALL-BUT-USELESS **MISSILE DEFENSE SYSTEM**--

--AND THEIR COMPLETE **CONTEMPT** FOR BASIC CIVIL LIBERTIES AND CONSTITUTIONAL RIGHTS--AND THEIR EFFORTS TO PORTRAY ANY DISSENT AS **UNPATRIOTIC**--AND--**AND**--

--SPLUTTER--

?

URK.

THUNK!

WHAT HAPPENED TO **HIM**?

OUTRAGE OVERLOAD. IT HAPPENS A LOT THESE DAYS.

--AND... ANOTHER THING...

THIS MODERN WORLD

by TOM TOMORROW

COMING SOON FROM BUSH ADMINISTRATION PRODUCTIONS-- THE THRILL-PACKED ACTION MOVIE EVENT OF THE SEASON--

LETHAL BUDDIES!

ONE GOES BY THE BOOK--THE *HOLY* BOOK!

THE OTHER PLAYS BY HIS *OWN* RULES!

THROWN TOGETHER WITH NOTHING IN COMMON BUT A *MUTUAL FOE*--AT FIRST, THEY *DESPISE* EACH OTHER AND BICKER *CONSTANTLY*--

ALL INFIDELS MUST DIE. THAT MEANS *YOU*, SOCIALIST PIG!

PUT A LID ON IT, CHUCKLES, OR YOU'LL BE MEETING ALLAH SOONER THAN YOU *EXPECTED*!

KA-BOOM!

KER-POW!

--BUT AS THE ACTION BUILDS, THEY BEGIN TO DEVELOP A *GRUDGING RESPECT* FOR ONE ANOTHER!

YOU'RE NOT SO BAD AFTER ALL--FOR A PSYCHOTIC RELIGIOUS ZEALOT, THAT IS!

AND YOU ARE TOLERABLE AS WELL--AS MURDEROUS PAGANS GO.

COULD IT BE THE START OF A *BEAUTIFUL FRIENDSHIP*?

I WILL WAIT TO OVERTHROW YOUR DECADENT REGIME UNTIL THE AMERICANS ARE DEFEATED, INFIDEL.

GREAT. AND I WON'T SEND YOU AND YOUR FOLLOWERS TO PARADISE *QUITE* YET.

CUT!! GUYS, IF YOU CAN'T DO BETTER THAN *THAT*, THE AUDIENCE IS *NEVER* GOING TO BELIEVE THIS SCRIPT!

FROM THE TOP! AND REMEMBER--YOU'RE SUPPOSED TO BE *BUDDIES!*

DIRECTOR

TOM TOMORROW©2-19-03

THIS MODERN WORLD

by TOM TOMORROW

CALL US CRAZY, BUT WE'VE RECENTLY BEGUN TO SUSPECT THAT SOME REMOTE VESTIGES OF RACISM **MAY** STILL EXIST IN OUR SOCIETY.

BUT--I THOUGHT WE TOOK CARE OF **THAT** WHEN TRENT LOTT WAS FORCED TO RESIGN AS SENATE MAJORITY LEADER!

YES--SURELY HIS DEMOTION TO MERE **UNITED STATES SENATOR** PROVED THAT WE DON'T TOLERATE **THAT** SORT OF THING ANYMORE!

FOR INSTANCE, NORTH CAROLINA CONGRESSMAN **HOWARD COBLE**--WHO IS, INCIDENTALLY, THE HEAD OF A HOUSE SUBCOMMITTEE ON CRIME, TERRORISM, AND HOMELAND SECURITY--RECENTLY SUGGESTED THAT THE INTERNMENT OF JAPANESE AMERICANS DURING WORLD WAR TWO WAS ACTUALLY A **GOOD** THING...

"THEY WERE AN **ENDANGERED SPECIES**...IT WASN'T SAFE FOR THEM TO BE ON THE **STREET!**"*

*ACTUAL QUOTE.

AND REPRESENTATIVE **SUE MYRICK**--ALSO FROM NORTH CAROLINA--LAST WEEK EXPRESSED THE FEARS SHE AND HER HUSBAND SHARE ABOUT THE DANGER AMERICA FACES FROM **WITHIN**...

"HONEST TO GOODNESS, ED AND I, FOR YEARS, FOR TWENTY YEARS, HAVE BEEN SAYING, 'YOU KNOW, LOOK AT WHO RUNS ALL THE CONVENIENCE STORES ACROSS THE COUNTRY!' EVERY LITTLE TOWN YOU GO INTO, YOU KNOW?"*

*YEP, ANOTHER ACTUAL QUOTE.

MEANWHILE...YOU PROBABLY DIDN'T HEAR ABOUT IT, BUT THE FBI IN SPOKANE JUST ARRESTED A COUPLE OF TERRORISTS FOR POSSESSION OF SECRET MILITARY DOCUMENTS--INCLUDING MATERIAL RELATING TO **CHEMICAL**, **NUCLEAR**, AND **BIOLOGICAL WARFARE**...

THAT'S **TERRIBLE!** WHO **WERE** THEY? **IRAQIS? AL QAEDA? HAMAS?**

UM--WHITE SUPREMACISTS, ACTUALLY.

OH--I THOUGHT YOU SAID THEY WERE **TERRORISTS.**

THE TERROR ALERTS REALLY **ARE** "COLOR CODED," AREN'T THEY?

YOU'RE MAKING ONE OF YOUR LITTLE POINTS HERE, AREN'T YOU?

TOM TOMORROW©2003...APOLOGIES TO MATT GROENING!

20

THIS MODERN WORLD

by TOM TOMORROW

NEW! FROM THE DEPARTMENT OF HOMELAND SECURITY...IT'S THE--

LOYAL AMERICAN'S GUIDE TO WAR PREPAREDNESS

WE'RE FROM THE GOVERNMENT!

WE'RE HERE TO *HELP!*

1. SPEND AS MUCH TIME AS POSSIBLE IN A STATE OF ACUTE BUT UNFOCUSED *ANXIETY!*

OH MY GOD--WHAT IF SADDAM HUSSEIN PLANTED A NUCLEAR DEVICE UNDER OUR *BED?!*

I'M--I'M SCARED TO *LOOK!*

2. IGNORE ANTI-WAR DEMONSTRATIONS, NO MATTER HOW *LARGE!*

MILLIONS OF PEOPLE GATHERED IN CITIES AROUND THE *WORLD!*

AH, BIG DEAL! THOSE NUMBERS ARE ALWAYS INFLATED ANYWAY!

3. ENTHUSIASTICALLY PROMOTE *PRO*-WAR DEMONSTRATIONS, NO MATTER HOW *SMALL!*

TWENTY PEOPLE IN PEORIA PROTESTED IN *FAVOR* OF THE WAR!

WELL--ALL RIGHT, THEN! THE AMERICAN PEOPLE HAVE *SPOKEN*--AND *THEY SUPPORT THE PRESIDENT!*

4. SHOW YOUR CONTEMPT FOR THE *FRENCH* AT EVERY OPPORTUNITY--LIKE THE DINER OWNER IN NORTH CAROLINA WHO NOW SERVES "FREEDOM FRIES" INSTEAD OF "*FRENCH* FRIES"!

AND WE NO LONGER CALL IT "FRENCH KISSING"--

--WE CALL IT "*FREEDOM* KISSING"!

5. FINALLY, IN THE EVENT OF RETALIATORY TERRORIST ATTACK, WELL, TRY TO BE SOMEWHERE ELSE.

YOU THINK *WE'RE* GONNA BE ANY HELP? CHRIST, IT'S TAKEN *US* A YEAR AND A HALF TO GET OUR *WEBSITE* UP AND RUNNING!

GO BUY SOME DUCT TAPE OR SOMETHING.

Department of Homeland Security

TOM TOMORROW©2003

21

THIS MODERN WORLD

by TOM TOMORROW

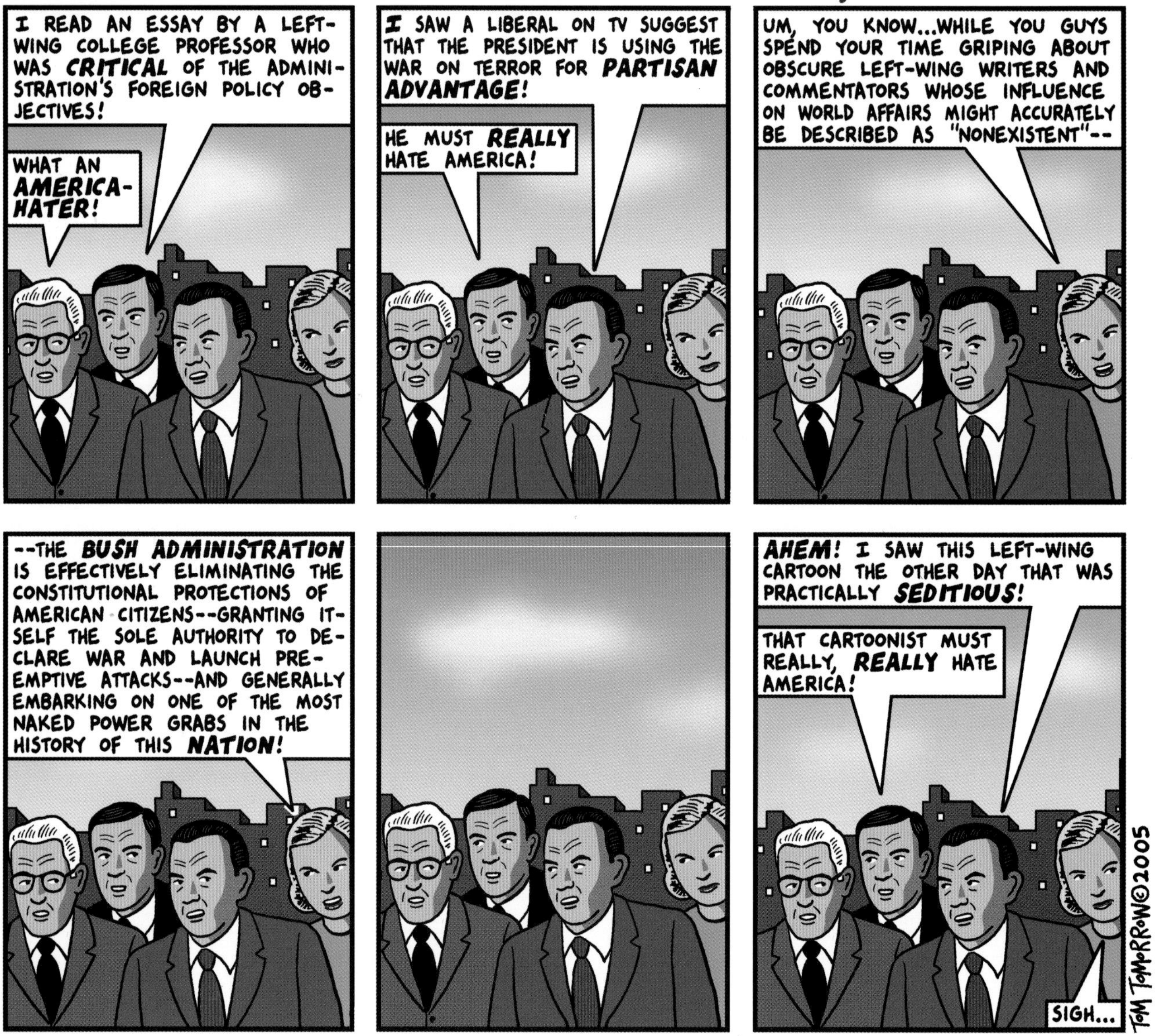

I READ AN ESSAY BY A LEFT-WING COLLEGE PROFESSOR WHO WAS *CRITICAL* OF THE ADMINISTRATION'S FOREIGN POLICY OBJECTIVES!
WHAT AN *AMERICA-HATER!*
I SAW A LIBERAL ON TV SUGGEST THAT THE PRESIDENT IS USING THE WAR ON TERROR FOR *PARTISAN ADVANTAGE!*
HE MUST *REALLY* HATE AMERICA!
UM, YOU KNOW...WHILE YOU GUYS SPEND YOUR TIME GRIPING ABOUT OBSCURE LEFT-WING WRITERS AND COMMENTATORS WHOSE INFLUENCE ON WORLD AFFAIRS MIGHT ACCURATELY BE DESCRIBED AS "NONEXISTENT"--
--THE *BUSH ADMINISTRATION* IS EFFECTIVELY ELIMINATING THE CONSTITUTIONAL PROTECTIONS OF AMERICAN CITIZENS--GRANTING ITSELF THE SOLE AUTHORITY TO DECLARE WAR AND LAUNCH PREEMPTIVE ATTACKS--AND GENERALLY EMBARKING ON ONE OF THE MOST NAKED POWER GRABS IN THE HISTORY OF THIS *NATION!*
AHEM! I SAW THIS LEFT-WING CARTOON THE OTHER DAY THAT WAS PRACTICALLY *SEDITIOUS!*
THAT CARTOONIST MUST REALLY, *REALLY* HATE AMERICA!
SIGH...
TOM TOMORROW©2005

THIS MODERN WORLD

by TOM TOMORROW

AS WE FIGHT THE WAR FORMERLY KNOWN AS THE WAR ON TERROR, AMERICANS MUST DECIDE...

HOW FAR IS TOO FAR?

WOULD IT BOTHER YOU AT ALL IF THE HOUSE UN-AMERICAN ACTIVITIES COMMITTEE RECONVENED AFTER ALMOST FIFTY YEARS AND SET OUT ON ANOTHER HOLLYWOOD *WITCH HUNT*?

CAN'T SAY THAT IT WOULD!

PATRIOTIC MOVIE STARS WOULD HAVE NOTHING TO FEAR!

WHAT IF NEW SEDITION LAWS WERE PASSED, MAKING CRITICISM OF THE GOVERNMENT A *PUNISHABLE OFFENSE*?

WELL, WE SHOULDN'T *BE* CRITICIZING THE GOVERNMENT AT A TIME LIKE THIS!

WE'RE EITHER WITH US-- OR WE'RE *AGAINST* US!

WOULD IT MAKE YOU UNEASY IF THE FBI WERE TO REVIVE ITS COINTELPRO ACTIVITY AND ATTEMPT TO UNDERMINE DISSENT THROUGH A CAMPAIGN OF *DIRTY TRICKS* AND *HARASSMENT*?

WHY ON EARTH *WOULD* IT?

IT'S NOT AS IF THEY'D BOTHER *LOYAL* AMERICANS!

WHAT IF AMERICAN CITIZENS OF MIDDLE EASTERN DESCENT WERE ROUNDED UP AND HELD IN *INTERNMENT CAMPS* FOR AN INDEFINITE DURATION?

IT WOULD BE UNFORTUNATE-- BUT WE *ARE* AT WAR!

I'M *SURE* THEY WOULD BE TREATED FAIRLY!

OR...WHAT IF THE ADMINISTRATION TRIED TO REDUCE OUR DEPENDENCE ON FOREIGN OIL BY ENACTING *STRICT FUEL EFFICIENCY STANDARDS*?

ARE YOU *KIDDING!?* *THAT* WOULD BE A BETRAYAL OF EVERYTHING THIS COUNTRY *STANDS FOR!!*

FREEDOM OF VEHICULAR CHOICE IS ONE OF OUR MOST *CHERISHED RIGHTS!!*

WHAT DO YOU THINK THIS *IS*-- NAZI GERMANY?!

IT *CAN'T* HAPPEN HERE--*CAN IT?!*

TOM TOMORROW©2002

THIS MODERN WORLD

by TOM TOMORROW

WE TRIED TO WARN YOU

SOME OF US UNDERSTOOD WHAT WAS AT STAKE...

IT'S BEEN **OBVIOUS** SINCE 9/11 THAT SADDAM THREATENS OUR VERY **WAY OF LIFE!**

HE HATES US BECAUSE WE ARE **FREE**, YOU KNOW!

?

...BUT TOO MANY OF **YOU** REFUSED TO **LISTEN!**

UM--YOU KNOW, I **STILL** DON'T QUITE SEE THE CONNECTION BETWEEN IRAQ AND **AL QAEDA**--

YEAH, YOU AND ALL YOUR FRIENDS IN THE "**AXIS OF WEASELS**"!

HA, HA! THAT GETS FUNNIER EVERY TIME I HEAR IT!

WELL, WE ALL KNOW WHAT HAPPENED **NEXT!**

YOUR ENDLESS DELAYS GAVE ME THE TIME I NEEDED TO DEVELOP A NEW MISSILE WITH A RANGE OF **SEVERAL** HUNDRED MILES!

BETWEEN THAT AND YOUR BALSA WOOD DRONE PLANES--WE HAVE NO **CHOICE** BUT TO SURRENDER!

HERE ARE THE KEYS TO THE WHITE HOUSE, OH MIGHTY CONQUEROR.

AND **THEN** THINGS WENT FROM BAD TO **WORSE!**

OSAMA, MY FRIEND--THE FIRST THING I WANT YOU TO DO AS HEAD OF THE OCCUPATIONAL AMERICAN GOVERNMENT IS ERADICATE THIS ACCURSED **FREEDOM** OF THEIRS!

BELIEVE ME, SADDAM, OLD BUDDY--IT'S NUMBER ONE ON MY "TO DO" LIST!

SO--AREN'T YOU SORRY YOU DIDN'T HEED OUR WARNINGS WHILE THERE WAS STILL **TIME**?

IF ONLY WE HAD LAUNCHED A MASSIVE PRE-EMPTIVE MILITARY STRIKE ON IRAQ BACK IN MARCH-- WE **MIGHT** STILL BE **FREE!**

WHAT FOOLS WE WERE TO QUESTION THE PRESIDENT-- ABOUT **ANYTHING!**

BE **SILENT**, SLAVES--OR SUFFER MY **WRATH!**

TOM TOMORROW©2003

THIS MODERN WORLD

by TOM TOMORROW

25

THIS MODERN WORLD

by TOM TOMORROW

THIS WEEK: DONALD RUMSFELD PLANS A DINNER PARTY!

FEATURING "DONALD'S LITTLE HELPERS"

RICKY PERLE-- AND PAULIE WOLFOWITZ!

SIR, THIS SIMPLY ISN'T ENOUGH *FOOD* FOR *ONE HUNDRED DIGNITARIES* AND THEIR *SPOUSES!*

NONSENSE! THEY'LL TAKE WHAT WE GIVE THEM--AND *LIKE* IT!

THEY'LL BE *GRATEFUL!*

NO QUESTION *ABOUT* IT!

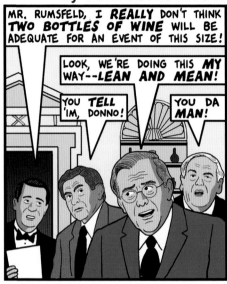

MR. RUMSFELD, I *REALLY* DON'T THINK *TWO BOTTLES OF WINE* WILL BE ADEQUATE FOR AN EVENT OF THIS SIZE!

LOOK, WE'RE DOING THIS *MY* WAY--*LEAN AND MEAN!*

YOU *TELL* 'IM, DONNO!

YOU DA *MAN!*

MR. SECRETARY, SIR, I *MUST* OBJECT! THIS SEATING PLAN WILL ONLY ACCOMODATE *TWENTY FIVE PEOPLE!*

YES, THAT'S RIGHT! I'M *TRYING* TO CONSERVE OUR RESOURCES FOR *FUTURE* DINNER PARTIES!

A *BRILLIANT* STRATEGY!

WHAT A VI-*SIONARY!*

SIR, THE GUESTS ARE *EXTREMELY* UNHAPPY.

WELL, FOR CHRISSAKES--WHY TELL *ME*? *YOU'RE* THE ONES WHO OR-*GANIZED* THIS MESS!

AND YOU'RE THE ONES WHO HAVE TO *DEAL* WITH IT!

OOPS! LOOK AT THE *TIME!* I, UM, HAVE TO GO.

TOM TOMORROW©2003

THIS MODERN WORLD

by TOM TOMORROW

ONCE AGAIN, IT'S TIME TO CHECK IN ON...
PARALLEL EARTH!

AS YOU MAY RECALL, A QUIRK IN THEIR ELECTION LAWS LED OUR INTERDIMENSIONAL COUNTERPARTS ON *PARALLEL EARTH* TO ELECT A *SMALL CUTE DOG* AS *THEIR* PRESIDENT TWO YEARS AGO.

ARF!

THEY'VE BEEN THROUGH A LOT IN PARALLEL AMERICA OVER THE LAST COUPLE OF YEARS...THEIR LATEST CRISIS BEGAN ONE DAY WHEN NO ONE REMEMBERED TO TAKE THE PRESIDENT OUT FOR HIS AFTERNOON *WALK*...

WHO LEFT THIS *MAP* LYING ON THE FLOOR? THE PRESIDENT HAS URINATED ON *LIECHTENSTEIN*!

HE'S CLEARLY MADE AN IMPORTANT *FOREIGN POLICY DECISION*!

THE PARALLEL ADMINISTRATION SOON TOOK ITS CASE TO THE *PUBLIC*...

THE PRESIDENT HAS DRAMATICALLY EXPRESSED HIS CONVICTION THAT LIECHTENSTEIN *MUST BE DEALT WITH*!

WHAT ARE THEY *HIDING* IN THEIR 62 *SQUARE MILES OF EVIL*?

BEFORE LONG, THE PARALLEL PUBLIC WAS *OBSESSED* BY A COUNTRY TO WHICH THEY'D GIVEN *LITTLE THOUGHT* IN THE RECENT PAST...

THOSE MORAL DEGENERATES REMAINED *NEUTRAL* DURING WORLD WAR TWO!

AND WHO *KNOWS* HOW MANY TERRORISTS LURK AMONG THEIR POPULATION OF 33,000 CITIZENS?

OTHER NATIONS OF PARALLEL EARTH WERE LESS ENTHUSIASTIC ABOUT THE WAR--AND WERE TREATED WITH APPROPRIATE *DERISION*...

I'D LIKE BELGIAN WAFFLES WITH CANADIAN BACON, PLEASE.

YOU MEAN *FREEDOM* WAFFLES WITH *LIBERTY* BACON?

UH-- SURE.

Menu

AND AS THE WAR BEGAN, THE PRESIDENT WAS ALREADY LOOKING AHEAD TO THE *NEXT* CHALLENGE.

THE PRESIDENT HAS *VOMITED* ON A MAP OF *AMERICAN SAMOA*! YOU KNOW WHAT *THAT* MEANS!

BUT--THAT'S A U.S. TERRITORY!

ARE YOU *QUESTIONING* THE *PRESIDENT*?

ER--NO, OF COURSE NOT! I'LL DRAW UP BATTLE PLANS RIGHT AWAY!

TOM TOMORROW©2003

27

THIS MODERN WORLD

by TOM TOMORROW

Panel 1: THE CDC ISSUES AN ADVISORY AS A MYSTERIOUS EPIDEMIC SWEEPS THE NATION...

STRENUOUSLY ASSERTIVE PATRIOTISM SYNDROME

MORE **FLAGS!**

NEED MORE **FLAGS!**

Panel 2: INITIAL SYMPTOMS OF **SAPS** RANGE FROM MANIC OPTIMISM TO CHRONIC PARANOIA--

YIPPEE! NOW THAT IRAQ HAS BEEN **LIBERATED**, A PEACE-LOVING, PRO-WESTERN DEMOCRACY IS **GUARANTEED** TO FLOURISH THERE!

BUT--WHAT ABOUT **SYRIA**? AND **IRAN**? THEY'RE **ALL** OUT TO **GET US**, YOU KNOW!

Panel 3: --AND ALMOST ALWAYS INCLUDE A PRONOUNCED AVERSION TO DIFFERING POINTS OF VIEW.

I'M JUST NOT CONVINCED THE ADMINISTRATION HAS BEEN ENTIRELY FORTHCOMING ABOUT ITS ULTIMATE **GOALS**--

GASP! GET **AWAY** FROM ME, YOU **TRAITOROUS PIG!**

HOW **DARE** YOU QUESTION OUR PRESIDENT AT A TIME LIKE THIS?!

Panel 4: IN ADVANCED CASES, THE MALADY CAN LEAD TO IRRATIONAL ANGER AND VIOLENT OUTBURSTS. CAUTION IS GREATLY ADVISED IN SUCH INSTANCES.

AMERICA--LOVE IT OR GET **RUN OVER**, THAT'S WHAT **I** ALWAYS SAY!

Panel 5: THE EPIDEMIC IS ALSO KNOWN TO INDUCE A STATE OF EXTREME **SUGGESTIBILITY**--RAISING CONCERNS THAT UNSCRUPULOUS INDIVIDUALS WILL TRY TO TAKE ADVANTAGE OF **SAPS**.

--SO YOU SEE, MY **TAX PLAN** WILL HELP **DEFEAT TERRORISM!**

I GUESS THE DEMOCRATS DON'T **WANT** TO DEFEAT TERRORISM!

Panel 6: FINALLY, WHILE NO CURE EXISTS AT THIS TIME, RISK OF EXPOSURE CAN BE MINIMIZED BY AVOIDING INFECTED MEDIA SOURCES. CABLE NEWS NETWORKS ARE PARTICULARLY CONTRAINDICATED.

FAIR AND BALANCED...GOD IS ON OUR SIDE... MUST SUPPORT THE PRESIDENT...

OH HONEY-- YOU'VE BEEN WATCHING FOX NEWS AGAIN, HAVEN'T YOU?

I'LL CALL THE DOCTOR.

TOM TOMORROW © 2003

THIS MODERN WORLD

by TOM TOMORROW

Panel 1: ACCORDING TO THE WALL STREET JOURNAL, THE BUSH ADMINISTRATION HAS *AUDACIOUS* PLANS TO WIN THE HEARTS AND MINDS OF THE IRAQI PEOPLE!

Panel 2: FOR INSTANCE, THEY WANT *EVERY CITIZEN* TO HAVE ACCESS TO *HEALTH CARE!* AND BECAUSE THEY'RE WORRIED ABOUT *RELIGIOUS FUNDAMENTALISTS* SETTING UP *PRIVATE SCHOOLS*--

Panel 3: --THEY'RE GOING TO SPEND *SIXTY-TWO MILLION DOLLARS* TO ESTABLISH A SECULAR, *GOVERNMENT-RUN* SCHOOL SYSTEM BY NEXT OCTOBER!

Panel 4: SO IN OTHER WORDS, UNIVERSAL HEALTH COVERAGE AND ADEQUATELY FUNDED PUBLIC SCHOOLS ARE AMONG OUR NATION'S TOP PRIORITIES--FOR *IRAQ*?

ABSOLUTELY! ALONG WITH *FREE AND FAIR ELECTIONS*, OF COURSE!

Panel 5:

Panel 6: AND THE IRONY OF ALL THIS IS, I ASSUME, COMPLETELY LOST ON YOU?

WHAT? YOU HAVE SOME SORT OF PROBLEM WITH *BASIC AMERICAN VALUES*?

TOM TOMORROW©2003

THIS MODERN WORLD

by TOM TOMORROW

WHAT GOES AROUND COMES AROUND

AN EXTREMELY TRUNCATED HISTORY OF REPUBLICANS, BECHTEL AND IRAQ

NOTE: THE INQUISITIVE READER WILL FIND A MORE COMPREHENSIVE OVERVIEW AT www.ips-dc.org

---

NOVEMBER, 1983: SECRETARY OF STATE (AND FORMER BECHTEL PRESIDENT) GEORGE SHULTZ RECEIVES AN INTELLIGENCE REPORT DESCRIBING SADDAM HUSSEIN'S "ALMOST DAILY" USE OF CHEMICAL WEAPONS. NO ACTION IS TAKEN.

HECK, WHAT'S A WAR CRIME OR TWO BETWEEN *FRIENDS*?

NOW--SOMEBODY GET ME *RUMSFELD*!

IN DECEMBER OF 1983, SPECIAL ENVOY DONALD RUMSFELD IS SENT TO MEET WITH SADDAM. THEY DISCUSS A POSSIBLE OIL PIPELINE FROM IRAQ TO JORDAN, TO BE CONSTRUCTED BY BECHTEL.

W.M.D.'S ARE NOT MENTIONED.

THE U.S. EVENTUALLY CONDEMNS IRAQ'S USE OF W.M.D.'S, BUT PIPELINE TALKS CONTINUE BEHIND THE SCENES UNTIL 1985, WHEN THE DEAL FALLS APART--REPORTEDLY BECAUSE SADDAM FEELS BECHTEL IS OVERPRICING THE JOB.

I JUST DON'T KNOW WHAT THE WORLD IS *COMING* TO--

--WHEN YOU CAN'T TRUST A POLITICALLY CONNECTED MULTINATIONAL CONTRACTOR TO CUT AN *HONEST BACKROOM DEAL* WITH A *TOTALITARIAN DICTATOR*!

STILL, BECHTEL DOES MANAGE TO SECURE A CONTRACT WITH SADDAM IN 1988--TO BUILD A HUGE *CHEMICAL PLANT* OUTSIDE OF BAGHDAD.

I'M *SURE* HE WILL USE IT FOR GOOD AND NOT EVIL.

ER--YES! RIGHT! ABSOLUTELY!

UNFORTUNATELY FOR BECHTEL, CONSTRUCTION IS HALTED AFTER IRAQ'S INVASION OF KUWAIT.

BUT--JUMP AHEAD TO APRIL, 2003! DONALD RUMSFELD IS SECRETARY OF DEFENSE, SADDAM IS HISTORY, AND GEORGE SHULTZ IS A BOARD MEMBER AT BECHTEL--WHICH HAS JUST BEEN AWARDED A *$680 MILLION IRAQ RECONSTRUCTION CONTRACT*!

SO YOU SEE, KIDS--GOOD THINGS *DO* COME TO THOSE WHO WAIT!

WHO *SAYS* THERE'S NO SUCH THING--

--AS A *HAPPY ENDING*?

TOM TOMORROW©2003

THIS MODERN WORLD

by TOM TOMORROW

BEFORE WE ALL GET DISTRACTED BY SYRIAN WEAPONS OF MASS DESTRUCTION AND THE OPPRESSION OF THE IRANIAN PEOPLE, LET'S PAUSE FOR A NOSTALGIC LOOK BACK AT--

THE LIBERATION OF IRAQ

featuring your hosts

Biff and Betty

1) THE TOPPLING OF THAT *STATUE!*

WHO CAN FORGET THE EXHILARATION WE ALL FELT WATCHING IT *OVER* AND *OVER* AND *OVER* *AGAIN*?

THE TIGHTLY-CROPPED CROWD SHOTS *REALLY* *ENHANCED* THE DRAMA OF THE MOMENT, IF YOU ASK *ME!*

2) CROWDS OF IRAQIS WAVING *AMERICAN FLAGS!*

WHERE DO YOU SUPPOSE THEY *GOT* ALL THOSE AMERICAN FLAGS, ANYWAY?

I'LL BET THEY'VE BEEN SECRETLY HOARDING THEM FOR *YEARS* IN ANTICIPATION OF THEIR INEVITABLE LIBERATION!

3) THE LIBERATION OF THE *SHI'ITES!*

THANKS TO *US,* THEY ARE NOW FREE TO PURSUE THEIR LONGSTANDING DREAM--

--THE ESTABLISHMENT OF AN ANTI-WESTERN *ISLAMIC* *THEOCRACY!*

4) THAT KID WITH *NO ARMS!*

WE KILLED HIS FAMILY AND CRIPPLED HIM FOR LIFE--BUT AT LEAST HE'LL GROW UP IN A *FREE SOCIETY!*

OR AN ISLAMIC THEOCRACY, DEPENDING ON HOW THINGS TURN OUT.

5) THE DOCTRINE OF *PRE-EMPTIVE WARFARE!*

IT WAS SUCH A SUCCESS, *INDIA* IS NOW CONSIDERING THEIR *OWN* PRE-EMPTIVE STRIKE AGAINST *PAKISTAN!*

IF THAT'S NOT *VALIDATION,* I DON'T KNOW WHAT *IS!*

COMING SOON: THE W.M.D.'S WE WENT TO WAR OVER ARE *FINALLY DISCOVERED,* UNLESS THEY'RE NOT.

TOM TOMORROW©2003

THIS MODERN WORLD

by TOM TOMORROW

Panel 1:
HEY, LIBERALS! DOES THE CURRENT REPUBLICAN STRANGLEHOLD ON ALL THREE BRANCHES OF GOVERNMENT FILL YOU WITH *DESPAIR*? WELL, *CHEER UP!* AT LEAST YOU CAN ALWAYS COUNT ON...

THE UNCOMPROMISING

LIBERAL MEDIA

Panel 2:
THEY'VE BEEN ON GEORGE BUSH'S CASE FROM *DAY ONE!* THANKS TO THEIR TIRELESS EFFORTS, THERE'S NOT A MAN, WOMAN OR CHILD IN THIS *COUNTRY* WHO REGARDS HIS PRESIDENCY AS *LEGITIMATE!*

EVERYONE KNOWS GORE WOULD HAVE WON AN *HONEST* RECOUNT!

AND WHAT ABOUT ALL THOSE BLACK VOTERS WHO WERE "ACCIDENTALLY" DROPPED FROM THE ROLLS?

Panel 3:
AND THEY'RE *STILL AT IT!* WHEN A WHITE HOUSE OFFICIAL OPENLY ACKNOWLEDGED THAT THE EVIDENCE FOR W.M.D.'S HAD BEEN OVERSTATED TO JUSTIFY WAR WITH IRAQ, THE MEDIA *COULD* HAVE BURIED THE STORY-- BUT OF *COURSE* THEY *DIDN'T!*

THE WHITE HOUSE TRIED TO MANIPULATE PUBLIC OPINION THROUGH *BLATANT FEAR-MONGERING!*

DID THEY THINK THE UNCOMPROMISING LIBERAL MEDIA WOULD LET THEM GET *AWAY* WITH IT?

Panel 4:
AND WHEN THE PRESIDENT STARTED PUSHING A DIVIDEND TAX CUT WHICH DISPROPORTIONATELY FAVORS THE RICH, THE UNCOMPROMISING LIBERAL MEDIA MADE *SURE* WE UNDERSTOOD THE DETAILS!

THE TOP ONE PERCENT WOULD RECEIVE AN AVERAGE OF ALMOST *TWELVE THOUSAND DOLLARS*--

--WHILE THE BOTTOM EIGHTY PERCENT GET ABOUT *THIRTY BUCKS!*

Panel 5:
AND THE LIBERAL MEDIA *CERTAINLY* WEREN'T GOING TO LET BUSH FLY TO THAT AIRCRAFT CARRIER TO GIVE HIS SPEECH--WITHOUT REMINDING US OF THE QUESTIONS SURROUNDING HIS *OWN* SERVICE RECORD!

AT THE HEIGHT OF THE VIETNAM WAR, HIS FAMILY PULLED STRINGS TO GET HIM INTO THE TEXAS AIR NATIONAL GUARD--

--AND EVEN THEN, HE SEEMS TO HAVE GONE *AWOL* FOR A YEAR OR SO!

Panel 6:
YES, THESE *ARE* HARD TIMES FOR LIBERALS...BUT REMEMBER: WITHOUT THE *UNCOMPROMISING LIBERAL MEDIA*, THINGS COULD BE A *WHOLE LOT WORSE*...

WHERE WOULD WE *BE* WITHOUT THEIR TIRELESS EFFORTS TO EXPOSE BUSH'S CHICANERY AND DECEIT?

I SHUDDER TO EVEN *CONSIDER* IT!

THANKS, LIBERAL MEDIA!

TOM TOMORROW©2003

THIS MODERN WORLD

by TOM TOMORROW

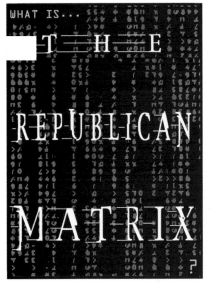

WHAT IS... THE REPUBLICAN MATRIX?

WHAT IS THE *REPUBLICAN MATRIX*? IT IS AN ILLUSION WHICH ENGULFS US ALL...A STEADY BARRAGE OF IMAGES WHICH OBSCURE REALITY...

BOY, DIDJA SEE THOSE PICTURES OF THE COMMANDER-IN-CHIEF IN A *FLIGHT SUIT*?

YOU *BET* I DID! I THINK FROM NOW ON WE SHOULD CALL HIM THE *HERO*-IN-CHIEF!

IT IS A WORLD BORN ANEW EACH DAY...IN WHICH THERE IS NOTHING TO BE LEARNED FROM THE LESSONS OF THE PAST...

A TAX CUT FOR THE RICH WILL CREATE *MILLIONS* OF NEW JOBS!

IS THAT HOW IT WORKED OUT TWO YEARS AGO?

I HAVE ABSOLUTELY NO IDEA WHAT YOU MIGHT BE TALKING ABOUT.

A WORLD WHERE LOGIC HOLDS NO SWAY...WHERE UP IS DOWN AND BLACK IS WHITE...

PRESIDENT BUSH IS WORKING TO *STRENGTHEN* ENVIRONMENTAL PROTECTION--

--BY *REPEALING* ENVIRONMENTAL *REGULATIONS!*

MAKES PERFECT SENSE TO *ME!*

WHERE REALITY ITSELF IS A MALLEABLE THING...SUBJECT TO CONSTANT REVISION...

IT DOESN'T MATTER IF WE FIND W.M.D.'S, BECAUSE WE *REALLY* WENT TO WAR TO FREE THE IRAQI PEOPLE!

EXCEPT, UM, IF WE DO FIND THEM. THEN THAT'S THE REASON AGAIN.

IN SHORT, IT'S *THEIR* WORLD-- WHAT SHOULD WE DO *TODAY*, FELLAS?

ANY DAMN THING WE WANT, GEORGE.

IS THIS A GREAT REALITY OR WHAT?

--WE'RE JUST TRAPPED IN IT.

TOM TOMORROW©2003

THIS MODERN WORLD

by TOM TOMORROW

LOVE 'EM OR HATE 'EM, ONE THING'S FOR SURE--THOSE BUSHIES ARE **MASTERS** OF IMAGE MANAGEMENT! FROM THEIR METICULOUSLY-PLANNED USE OF NATIONAL LANDMARKS AND OTHER PATRIOTIC SETTINGS--

HOW'S THIS LOOK, KARL?

VERY PRESIDENTIAL, SIR.

YOUR PHOTO ON MOUNT RUSHMORE $5.00

--TO THE UBIQUITOUS BACKDROP SLOGANS WHICH **SUBTLY UNDERSCORE** THE PRESIDENT'S MESSAGE OF THE DAY--NO DETAIL IS **OVERLOOKED!**

--AND THAT IS WHY DEMOCRATS MUST **CEASE** THEIR FUTILE OPPOSITION--AND INSTEAD **WORSHIP ME LIKE A GOD!!**

Worship the President, Puny Mortals

Worship the President, Puny Mortals

Worship the President, Puny Mortals

AND OF COURSE, THEY **REALLY** OUTDID THEMSELVES WITH THAT PHOTO OP ON THE **AIRCRAFT CARRIER!**

ARI, IS IT TRUE THAT THE PRESIDENT CHARTED THE COURSE, PILOTED THE JET, AND LANDED IT **HIMSELF?**

WELL, UH--LET'S JUST SAY THAT THE WHITE HOUSE HAS NO PLANS TO DISABUSE YOU OF THAT NOTION.

THE ONLY PROBLEM THEY'VE GOT **NOW**...IS WHAT TO DO FOR AN **ENCORE!**

OKAY--AFTER AN EXCITING SHOOTOUT WITH AL QAEDA HENCHMEN ON THE **SKI SLOPE**, YOU JUMP OFF THE **CLIFF**, OPEN A **PARACHUTE** EMBLAZONED WITH AN **AMERICAN FLAG**...AND LAND IN FRONT OF A GROUP OF REPORTERS WAITING AT THE **BOTTOM!**

CAN I DODGE SOME BULLETS IN **SLOW MOTION**? THAT WOULD BE **REALLY** COOL!

I'LL LOOK INTO IT, SIR.

BAD GUY

POTUS (fig. b)

POTUS (fig. a)

MEDIA

TOM TOMORROW©2003

34

THIS MODERN WORLD

by TOM TOMORROW

THIS MODERN WORLD

by TOM TOMORROW

FEAR FACTOR

You LIVED IN DREAD OF OSAMA BIN LADEN.

I'LL BET HE IS OMNISCIENT AND OMNIPRESENT--LIKE A *JAMES BOND SUPERVILLAIN!*

WHO *KNOWS* WHERE HE WILL STRIKE NEXT!

YOU WERE TERRIFIED OF YOUR OWN MAIL.

THE PUBLISHER'S CLEARINGHOUSE LETTER DOESN'T APPEAR TO CONTAIN ANY POWDERY SUBSTANCES!

THIS NOTICE FROM THE *I.R.S.* LOOKS SUSPICIOUS! WE'D BETTER BURN *IT*-- JUST TO BE *SAFE!*

YOU HAD NIGHTMARES ABOUT SADDAM HUSSEIN.

WHAT IF HE LAUNCHES A FIRST STRIKE NUCLEAR ATTACK?

HE *DOES* HAVE MISSILES CAPABLE OF TRAVELLING *SEVERAL MILES!*

YOU STOCKED UP ON DUCT TAPE AND PLASTIC SHEETING.

OKAY, THE HOUSE IS NOW *COMPLETELY AIRTIGHT!* WE SHOULD BE SAFE *NOW!*

AS LONG AS OUR OXYGEN HOLDS OUT, AT LEAST!

LATELY, YOU MIGHT BE THINKING THAT THINGS HAVE CALMED DOWN AND YOU CAN RELAX A LITTLE...

HEY, WHAT'S THE DEAL WITH THAT *TAX CUT*, ANYWAY? DON'T WE HAVE A HUGE *DEFICIT* RIGHT NOW?

YEAH--AND THERE'S NO TELLING *WHAT* THE RECONSTRUCTION OF IRAQ IS GOING TO COST US!

WELL, THINK AGAIN.

NEVER MIND ALL *THAT!* HAVEN'T YOU HEARD ABOUT *NORTH KOREA'S NUCLEAR PROGRAM?* AND *SYRIA'S W.M.D.'S?* AND *SARS?* AND--AND--

HE'S *RIGHT!* WE'RE DOOMED! WE'RE ALL *DOOMED!*

SOMEBODY, PLEASE-- MAKE IT *STOP!*

AND ON AND ON AND ON IT GOES...

TOM TOMORROW©2003

THIS MODERN WORLD

by TOM TOMORROW

Panel 1:
WHO WILL THE DEMOCRATS NOMINATE IN 2004?

RUDE AND AGGRESSIVE *GOOFUS*--

--OR CONSIDERATE, WELL-MANNERED *GALLANT*?

Panel 2:
CANDIDATE *GOOFUS* CHALLENGES THE PRESIDENT'S RECORD ON TERRORISM!

--WHILE *HE'S* BEEN BUSY INVADING UNRELATED COUNTRIES, AL QAEDA HAS *REGROUPED*--LEAVING US MORE VULNERABLE THAN *EVER!*

GooFus foR PreSiDenT

Panel 3:
CANDIDATE *GALLANT* POLITELY SUGGESTS WAYS IN WHICH THE PRESIDENT COULD DO AN EVEN *BETTER* JOB!

--AND SO, IF WE BEEF UP SECURITY AT CERTAIN ENTRY POINTS, WE'LL BE *EVEN SAFER* THAN WE ARE *NOW!*

GaLLanT foR PreSiDenT

Panel 4:
CANDIDATE GOOFUS REPEATEDLY BRINGS UP UNPLEASANT TOPICS SUCH AS *ECONOMIC DISPARITY!*

MILLIONS OF JOBS HAVE BEEN LOST--AND ALL GEORGE BUSH WANTS TO DO IS GIVE HIS *RICH BUDDIES* ANOTHER *TAX CUT!*

GooFus foR PreSiDenT

Panel 5:
CANDIDATE GALLANT DOESN'T WANT TO BE ACCUSED OF *CLASS WARFARE!*

I BELIEVE A PROGRAM OF *MILD* AND *INCREMENTAL REFORM* WILL EVENTUALLY MAKE THIS COUNTRY A *SLIGHTLY BETTER PLACE* THAN IT IS TODAY!

GaLLanT foR

Panel 6:
CANDIDATE GOOFUS TAKES CONTROL OF THE TERMS OF THE DEBATE--WITHOUT ASKING *ANYONE'S* PERMISSION!

PRESIDENT BUSH *MUST* ANSWER TO THE AMERICAN PEOPLE FOR THE COUNTLESS FAILURES OF HIS ADMINISTRATION!

GooFus foR

Panel 7:
CANDIDATE GALLANT RESPONDS TO EACH NEW REPUBLICAN ATTACK IN A *PATIENT* AND *REASONABLE MANNER!*

GOLLY, I SURE DON'T KNOW HOW THESE RUMORS GET STARTED--BUT I REALLY *DON'T* SPEND MY EVENINGS BURNING AMERICAN FLAGS WHILE MEMORIZING PASSAGES FROM *DAS KAPITAL!* HONEST!

GaLLanT foR

Panel 8:
SO WHO WILL THE DEMOCRATS *SUPPORT?*

GEE WHIZ--WE *CAN'T* RUN A McGOVERNITE ELITIST LIKE *GOOFUS!*

NO DOUBT ABOUT IT--GALLANT IS *CLEARLY* A MORE ELECTABLE CANDIDATE!

DeMocRatic LeaDership CouNciL

STAY TUNED...

TOM TOMORROW ©2003

THIS MODERN WORLD

by TOM TOMORROW

THE revised OFFICIAL BUSH ADMINISTRATION HISTORY OF THE WAR ON IRAQ

DICK CHENEY, SPEECH TO V.F.W. CONVENTION, AUGUST 26, 2002:

"SIMPLY STATED, THERE IS **NO DOUBT** THAT SADDAM HAS two tractor trailers which could conceivably be used to produce WEAPONS OF MASS DESTRUCTION!"

DONALD RUMSFELD, PRESS BRIEFING, FEBRUARY 19, 2003:

"WHAT WE'RE TALKING ABOUT HERE IS THE POTENTIAL FOR two tractor trailers of indeterminate purpose TO BE USED AGAINST OUR COUNTRY!"

COLIN POWELL, RADIO INTERVIEW, FEBRUARY 28, 2003:

"IF IRAQ HAD...GOTTEN RID OF ITS two tractor trailers which with some modifications could possibly be used to manufacture WEAPONS OF MASS DESTRUCTION... WE WOULD NOT BE FACING THE CRISIS THAT WE NOW HAVE BEFORE US!"

GEORGE W. BUSH, ADDRESS TO THE NATION, MARCH 17, 2003:

"INTELLIGENCE GATHERED BY THIS AND OTHER GOVERNMENTS LEAVES NO DOUBT THAT THE IRAQ REGIME CONTINUES TO POSSESS two OF THE MOST LETHAL tractor trailers EVER **DEVISED!**"

SO THERE YOU HAVE IT--THE BUSH ADMINISTRATION WAS **RIGHT ALL ALONG!**

THE AMERICAN PEOPLE are truly fortunate to have leaders of such caliber!

I, FOR ONE, hope that the President is re-elected in a landslide!

38

THIS MODERN WORLD

by TOM TOMORROW

Panel 1: AFTER THE ARREST OF ERIC RUDOLPH, HOMELAND SECURITY RAISES THE TERROR LEVEL TO "HIGH".

WE'VE GOT TO BE *ALERT!* THERE ARE STILL PLENTY OF *OTHER* CHRISTIAN TERRORISTS OUT THERE!

WHAT KIND OF RELIGION TEACHES ITS ADHERENTS TO PLANT PIPE BOMBS IN THE MIDDLE OF THE OLYMPICS *ANYWAY?*

Panel 2: THE PRESIDENT REMINDS THE NATION THAT *CHRISTIANS* ARE NOT THE ENEMY.

WE'RE AT WAR WITH *TERRORISM*-- NOT ANY SPECIFIC RELIGION!

MANY CHRISTIANS ARE ACTUALLY DECENT, LAW-ABIDING FOLKS-- JUST LIKE YOU AND *ME!*

Christians: not all bad! Christians: not all bad! Christians: not all bad! Christians: not all bad! Christians: not all bad! Christians: not all bad! Christians: not all bad!

Panel 3: STILL, THE JUSTICE DEPARTMENT BEGINS SURVEILLANCE OF KNOWN CHRISTIAN GATHERING PLACES.

THEY'RE IN THERE SINGING ABOUT THE "BLOOD OF THE LAMB."

MUST BE SOME SORT OF CODED MESSAGE FOR THEIR SLEEPER AGENTS.

Panel 4: HUNDREDS OF CHRISTIANS ARE INDEFINITELY DETAINED WITHOUT ACCESS TO LEGAL COUNSEL.

IF THEIR INNOCENCE IS ESTABLISHED AFTER MULTIPLE INTERROGATIONS OVER A PERIOD OF PROLONGED INCARCERATION--THEN THEY'LL BE RELEASED.

PROBABLY.

I DON'T SEE WHY ANYONE SHOULD HAVE A PROBLEM WITH *THAT.*

Panel 5: MEANWHILE, TV PUNDITS ARGUE ABOUT WHETHER OR NOT CHRISTIANITY IS A *PEACEFUL* RELIGION.

THE CHRISTIAN SAVIOR ESPOUSED A MESSAGE OF *NON-VIOLENCE.*

YEAH, WELL--TELL IT TO THE VICTIMS OF THE OLYMPIC PARK *BOMBING!*

AND HAVE YOU *HEARD* OF THE CRUSADES?

Panel 6: AND THE U.S. MILITARY BEGINS A TROOP DEPLOYMENT ALONG THE BORDER OF THE SO-CALLED "BIBLE BELT."

WE'VE GOT TO INVADE THEIR COUNTIES, KILL THEIR LEADERS, AND CONVERT THEM ALL TO *SECULAR HUMANISM!*

IT'S THE ONLY WAY TO *WIN* THIS WAR!

TOM TOMORROW ©2003

THIS MODERN WORLD

by TOM TOMORROW

LET'S HOLD THE REPUBLICAN CONVENTION IN SUBURBAN CHICAGO, NEAR THE FORMER HOME OF CHILD MOLESTING SERIAL KILLER *JOHN WAYNE GACY*-- TO EMPHASIZE YOUR CONCERN FOR THE *YOUTH* OF AMERICA!

ARE YOU *CRAZY*? THAT'S A *TERRIBLE* IDEA!

WELL, WHAT IF WE HAVE IT NEAR THE HOSPITAL WHERE RICHARD SPECK KILLED ALL THOSE NURSES-- TO UNDERSCORE YOUR COMMITMENT TO *QUALITY HEALTH CARE*?

WHAT THE HECK HAVE YOU BEEN *SMOKIN'*, KARL?

OKAY--WE COULD GO DOWN TO *GUYANA*, WHERE ALL THE FOLLOWERS OF CULT LEADER JIM JONES COMMITTED MASS SUICIDE--IN ORDER TO HIGHLIGHT *YOUR* ADHERENCE TO *TRADITIONAL* RELIGIOUS VALUES!

WHAT IS *WITH* YOU GUYS? DO YOU WANT PEOPLE TO THINK WE'RE A BUNCH OF *GHOULS*?

I KNOW! LET'S HAVE OUR CONVENTION IN *NEW YORK CITY*, CLOSE TO THE ANNIVERSARY OF THE 9/11 ATTACKS--TO SYMBOLIZE YOUR DEVOTION TO A *SAFE* AND *PROSPEROUS AMERICA*!

NOW YOU'RE *TALKIN'*!

YOU THINK WE COULD FIND SOME *WIDOWS* AND *ORPHANS* TO BRING UP ON STAGE?

I'M SURE OF IT, SIR.

TOM TOMORROW©2003

THIS MODERN WORLD

by TOM TOMORROW

THE PRESIDENT'S CRITICS ACCUSE HIM OF *LYING* ABOUT THE THREAT POSED BY IRAQ BEFORE THE WAR--BUT WAS IT REALLY A *LIE* IF HE *BELIEVED* WHAT HE WAS SAYING AT THE *TIME*?

GOOD POINT!

day *table* Sunday Roundtable *Sun* *Roun*

OR WHAT IF HE *DIDN'T* BELIEVE WHAT HE WAS SAYING--BUT DIDN'T EXPECT *US* TO, EITHER? I DON'T KNOW IF *THAT* WOULD TECHNICALLY CONSTITUTE A *LIE*!

NO HARM, NO FOUL--THAT'S WHAT *I* SAY!

day *table* Sunday Roundtable *Sun* *Round*

OR MAYBE HE *DID* EXAGGERATE THE EVIDENCE *SLIGHTLY*--BUT WITH THE *BEST OF INTENTIONS*! WOULDN'T THAT REALLY BE MORE OF A *LITTLE WHITE LIE*? AND WHO AMONG US HASN'T TOLD ONE OF *THOSE*?

SOMETIMES YOU *HAVE* TO STRETCH THE TRUTH A *LITTLE*!

table *Re* *ndtable* *Sunda* *Roundta*

OR--WHAT IF HE *DELIBERATELY DECEIVED* AMERICANS BECAUSE HE KNEW THEY'D NEVER SUPPORT SENDING THEIR SONS AND DAUGHTERS TO DIE IN PURSUIT OF SOME NEO-CON WET DREAM OF GLOBAL HEGE-MONY? WOULD *THAT* TRULY BE CONSIDERED A *LIE*?

day *table* Sunday Roundtable *Sund* *Round*

COUGH!

AHEM!

nday *ndtable* *unday* *Roundtable* *Su* *Roun*

I GUESS IT WOULD, HUH?

MOVING RIGHT ALONG TO OUR *NEXT* TOPIC--*HILLARY'S NEW BOOK*! IS IT FULL OF *LIES* OR *WHAT*?

FIRST THESE MESSAGES.

nday *ndtable* Sunday Roundtable *Sur* *Roun*

TOM TOMORROW©2003

THIS MODERN WORLD

by TOM TOMORROW

SEPT. 11 1998: THE DAY EVERYTHING CHANGED

AFTER THE TERRORIST ATTACKS, AMERICANS IMMEDIATELY SET THEIR POLITICAL DIFFERENCES ASIDE.

THIS IS A *NEW* KIND OF WAR, FELLAS--A WAR ON *TERROR!*

WE'LL STAND BEHIND YOU *NO MATTER WHAT*, MR. PRESIDENT!

CONGRESSIONAL REPUBLICANS QUICKLY ABANDONED THEIR IMPEACHMENT EFFORTS.

WHO CARES ABOUT THE PRESIDENT'S *SEX LIFE*, FOR CHRISSAKES?

WE'VE GOT MORE *IMPORTANT* THINGS TO WORRY ABOUT *NOW!*

FOX NEWS RALLIED BEHIND THE PRESIDENT'S CALL FOR AMERICA TO WEAN ITSELF FROM ITS DEPENDENCE ON MIDEAST OIL.

IF THE COMMANDER-IN-CHIEF SAYS WE SHOULD DRIVE *SMALLER CARS*--

--THEN BY GOD, IT'S THE *PATRIOTIC THING TO DO!*

TALKING POINTS...

Good Americans SUPPORT the President!

BEFORE LONG, RUSH LIMBAUGH MADE A STUNNING ANNOUNCEMENT.

YOU SEE, LADIES AND GENTLEMEN, I SIMPLY DON'T FEEL THAT ANYONE SHOULD *EVER* CRITICIZE A SITTING PRESIDENT--OR EVEN HIS POLITICAL PARTY--IN A TIME OF WAR!

AND SO IN THE BEST INTERESTS OF OUR COUNTRY, *I* HAVE DECIDED TO *RETIRE!*

AND FOR THE REST OF HIS TERM, THE PRESIDENT PURSUED A PARTISAN AGENDA IN THE NAME OF NATIONAL SECURITY--AND NARY A PEEP WAS HEARD FROM HIS CRITICS.

NO QUESTION ABOUT IT, GENTLEMEN-- THESE ANTHRAX ATTACKS *PROVE* THE NEED FOR *UNIVERSAL HEALTH COVERAGE!*

ANYTHING YOU SAY, SIR!

WE'RE WITH YOU ALL THE WAY!

TOM TOMORROW©2005

THIS MODERN WORLD

by TOM TOMORROW

Panel 1: --AND ACCORDING TO A SENIOR WHITE HOUSE OFFICIAL, YOU CAN'T SUPPORT THE *TROOPS* UNLESS YOU SUPPORT THE *PRESIDENT*--AND HEAVEN KNOWS, WE ALL WANT TO SUPPORT THE *TROOPS!* RIGHT, BIFF?

I CAN'T STAND IT ANYMORE.

ER--BIFF?

Panel 2: WANDA, WE IN THE NEWS MEDIA ARE SO *SPINELESS*, SO AFRAID OF BETRAYING SOME HINT OF LIBERAL *BIAS*, THAT WE'LL PRETTY MUCH SAY ANYTHING THE ADMINISTRATION *TELLS* US TO SAY--AND *I CAN'T STAND IT ANYMORE!*

Panel 3: YOU WANT TO KNOW HOW PRESIDENT *AWOL* SUPPORTS THE TROOPS? APART FROM STRUTTING AROUND IN A PADDED *FLIGHT SUIT*, I MEAN? BY SLASHING *VETERANS' BENEFITS* TO THE *BONE!* BY TRYING TO CUT THEIR "*IMMINENT DANGER*" PAY FROM A PALTRY $225 A MONTH TO AN EVEN *MORE* PALTRY $150!

Panel 4: HE'S EVEN OPPOSED TO A PLAN WHICH WOULD DOUBLE THE MEAGER $6,000 CURRENTLY PAID TO THE FAMILIES OF TROOPS *KILLED* WHILE ON ACTIVE DUTY! BUT HEY--*HE* NEEDS THE MONEY TO GIVE HIS RICH BUDDIES ANOTHER HUGE *TAX BREAK*--AND--AND--

URK!

Panel 5: TECHNICAL DIFFICULTIES — PLEASE STAND BY

Panel 6: THIS JUST IN: LOCAL NEWS ANCHOR REVEALED TO BE AN OPERATIVE OF *AL QAEDA!*

WE'LL HAVE THE *SHOCKING DETAILS* AFTER *THESE MESSAGES!*

TOM TOMORROW ©2003

43

THIS MODERN WORLD

by TOM TOMORROW

FOREIGN POLICY MADE E-Z

MANY AMERICANS WERE STARTLED WHEN THE PRESIDENT SEEMED TO **DARE** ENEMY COMBATANTS TO ATTACK U.S. MILITARY PERSONNEL...

THERE ARE SOME WHO FEEL LIKE THAT, YOU KNOW, THE CONDITIONS ARE SUCH THAT THEY CAN ATTACK US THERE. MY ANSWER IS, **BRING 'EM ON!***

*ACTUAL QUOTE.

...BUT HIS SUPPORTERS QUICKLY EXPLAINED WHAT HE **REALLY** MEANT!

WHAT APPEARED TO BE MINDLESS BELLICOSITY WAS ACTUALLY PART OF A **CAREFULLY CONCEIVED STRATEGY!**

THAT'S RIGHT! YOU SEE, THE PRESIDENT, IS DELIBERATELY **USING** THE ONGOING CONFLICT IN IRAQ TO LURE THE **TERRORISTS** OUT INTO THE **OPEN!***

*ACTUAL ARGUMENT MAKING THE ROUNDS IN CONSERVATIVE CIRCLES.

WE SURE HOPE OUR SERVICEMEN AND WOMEN IN IRAQ ARE PAYING ATTENTION TO THESE ARMCHAIR STRATEGISTS--BECAUSE WE CAN'T **THINK** OF A BETTER MORALE BOOSTER!

HEY GUYS, ACCORDING TO THIS ARTICLE, WE'RE DOING A GREAT JOB HERE--AS **BAIT!**

NOW THAT'S WHAT **I** CALL SUPPORTING THE **TROOPS!**

AND CLEARLY THE PRESIDENT'S PLAN IS **WORKING!** AFTER ALL, THERE HASN'T BEEN A TERRORIST ATTACK IN THE U.S. SINCE HE **MADE** HIS REMARKS!

WE ARE READY TO PROCEED WITH OUR PLOT TO DESTROY THE BROOKLYN BRIDGE!

NEVER MIND **THAT!** DID YOU NOT HEAR THE INFIDEL BUSH'S PROVOCATIVE STATEMENT? WE MUST CATCH THE FIRST PLANE TO **BAGHDAD!**

YES, IT JUST PROVES ONCE AGAIN THAT WHEN IT COMES TO THE BUSH ADMINISTRATION, **FAILURE** IS JUST ANOTHER WORD FOR **SUCCESS!**

GREAT NEWS! THERE WAS **ANOTHER** ATTACK ON AMERICAN TROOPS IN IRAQ TODAY!

THAT'S TERRIFIC! AT THIS RATE, THE PRESIDENT'S GONNA HAVE TO DECLARE VICTORY **ALL OVER AGAIN!**

TOM TOMORROW©2003

44

THIS MODERN WORLD

by TOM TOMORROW

THE STORY: SADDAM TRIED TO BUY URANIUM FROM NIGER. REFERENCED IN STATE OF THE UNION ADDRESS TO HIGHLIGHT IMMINENT THREAT POSED BY IRAQ.

DON'T THOSE IDIOT PEACENIKS UNDERSTAND WHAT'S AT *STAKE* HERE?

HOW MUCH EVIDENCE DO THEY *NEED*?

MORE TO THE STORY: THE CIA CONSIDERED THE ASSERTION DUBIOUS AT BEST--AND IT'S EXTREMELY UNLIKELY THAT THE PRESIDENT WAS UNAWARE OF THIS AT THE TIME.

OH.

AHEM.

THE STORY: "ONLY 33" PIECES WERE LOOTED FROM THE IRAQI NATIONAL MUSEUM. USED BY BUSH SYCOPHANTS TO DISCREDIT EARLIER REPORTS OF MUCH MORE MASSIVE LOOTING.

HA, HA! THE LIBERALS WERE AS WRONG ABOUT *THAT* AS THEY ARE ABOUT *EVERYTHING*!

I THINK THEY SHOULD PUBLICLY DENOUNCE *THEMSELVES*--AS *MORONS*!

MORE TO THE STORY: AS OF THIS WRITING, AT LEAST 13,000 PIECES HAVE BEEN REPORTED MISSING OR DESTROYED. ADDITIONALLY, THE IRAQI NATIONAL LIBRARY WAS BURNED TO THE GROUND, AND LOOTING APPARENTLY CONTINUES AT ARCHEOLOGICAL SITES THROUGHOUT IRAQ.

OH.

AHEM.

THE STORY: U.S. TROOPS LIBERATED A PRISON FULL OF CHILDREN WHO HAD REFUSED TO JOIN THE BAATH PARTY YOUTH GROUP. USED TO UNDERSCORE THE MORAL NECESSITY OF OUR PRE-EMPTIVE INVASION.

ONCE AGAIN, THE PRESIDENT HAS BEEN *VINDICATED*!

ONLY A *DEPRAVED LEFTIST* COULD *DISPUTE* IT!

MORE TO THE STORY: THE NEW YORK TIMES REPORTS THAT THE "PRISON" WAS ACTUALLY AN ORPHANAGE--AND MANY OF THE ORPHANS WE "LIBERATED" ARE NOW LIVING ON THE STREET, BEGGING AND POSSIBLY PROSTITUTING THEMSELVES TO SURVIVE...

OH.

AHEM.

AND ON AND ON AND ON IT GOES...

TOM TOMORROW©2003

THIS MODERN WORLD

BY TOM TOMORROW

IN THE MONTH OF MARCH, IN THE YEAR OF OUR LORD 2003, AS THE WAR IN IRAQ WAS JUST ABOUT TO COMMENCE, I COMPLETED WORK ON MY *TIME MACHINE*--AND EMBARKED ON A JOURNEY TO VIEW THE INEVITABLY TRIUMPHANT *RESOLUTION* OF THAT CONFLICT...

I SET MY DEVICE TO TAKE ME A CAUTIOUS *THREE WEEKS* INTO THE FUTURE...NOTHING SEEMED DIFFERENT--BUT WHEN I TURNED ON THE TELEVISION, I DISCOVERED, TO MY ASTONISHMENT, THAT A SWIFT VICTORY HAD *ALREADY BEEN ACHIEVED!*

THUS EMBOLDENED, I TRAVELLED SEVERAL *MONTHS* AHEAD...AND UPON MY ARRIVAL IN THIS DISTANT FUTURE, I VENTURED OUT ONTO THE STREET AND BRACED THE FIRST PASSERBY I SAW...

PRAY FORGIVE THE INTRUSION, KIND SIR, BUT CAN YOU TELL ME--

--HOW GOES THE RESTORATION OF IRAQ? HAVE SADDAM'S VAST STOCK-PILES OF UNIMAGINABLY DESTRUCTIVE WEAPONS BEEN LOCATED AND *SECURED*? IS THE GRATITUDE OF THE LIBERATED IRAQI POPULACE SO EXCESSIVE AS TO BE *UNSEEMLY*? AND IS IRAQ YET A SHINING BEACON OF DEMOCRACY--OR SIMPLY *WELL ON THE WAY*?

?

THIS MAN OF THE FUTURE REGARDED ME STRANGELY--AND THEN BEGAN TO PAINT A PORTRAIT SO RELENTLESSLY GRIM, I COULD SCARCELY BELIEVE MY *EARS*...

LOOTING AND CHAOS...

YELLOWCAKE URANIUM SCANDAL...

NO W.M.D.'S...

INDEFINITE OCCUPATION...

DAILY FATALITIES...

NO-- NO-- IT *CAN'T BE!*

I QUICKLY RETURNED TO MY TIME, BUT MY CONTEMPORARIES PROVED QUITE UNWILLING TO HEED MY WARNINGS...AND WHO CAN *BLAME* THEM? IT ALL MADE SUCH *PERFECT SENSE* AT THE *TIME*...

LISTEN--WE'RE GONNA LIBERATE THE IRAQIS, FIND THE W.M.D.'S, SET UP A FUNCTIONING DEMOCRACY--AND WE'RE *OUT* OF THERE!

I FIGURE A COUPLE OF MONTHS, TOPS!

AND YOU'RE EITHER *WITH* US--OR YOU'RE *OBJECTIVELY PRO-SADDAM!* GOT IT?

SIGH...

TOM TOMORROW©2003

THIS MODERN WORLD

by TOM TOMORROW

Panel 1: EVER SINCE THE PASSAGE OF THE 28TH AMENDMENT (MANDATING THAT THE PRESIDENT OF THE U.S. MUST ALWAYS BE A MEMBER OF THE BUSH FAMILY), WE'VE HAD **REAL STABILITY** IN THIS COUNTRY!

I WONDER WHAT IT WOULD BE LIKE NOT TO HAVE A **BUSH** IN THE WHITE HOUSE!

QUIET! YOU WANNA GET ARRESTED FOR **SEDITION**?

Panel 2: IN 2008, JEB TOOK OVER...AND IN 2016, THEY LET **NEIL** OUT OF WHATEVER ATTIC THEY'D BEEN HIDING HIM IN SINCE THE S&L SCANDALS...WHICH ULTIMATELY DIDN'T WORK OUT SO WELL...

NEIL **FREE** NOW! NEIL WANT **MEAT**! AND **WOMAN**!

WE'LL, UH, GET RIGHT ON THAT, SIR.

Panel 3: THEN IT WAS THE TWINS' TURN... HAVING LONG SINCE RENOUNCED THE EXCESSES OF THEIR YOUTH, THEY ARE REMEMBERED PRIMARILY FOR REINSTATING **PROHIBITION**, WITH THE **ANTI-TERRORISM HANGOVER ELIMINATION ACT** OF 2029...

YOU'RE EITHER **WITH** US--OR WE'LL TURN ON YOU LIKE A DRUNK ON A **THREE DAY BINGE**!

AND BELIEVE YOU ME-- WE KNOW **HOW**!

PRAISE **JESUS**!

Panel 4: THE NEXT FEW DECADES WERE PROBLEMATIC FOR THE BUSH DYNASTY... BY THE TIME MAD **LUDWIG BUSH** TOOK COMMAND OF THE OVAL OFFICE, IT WAS CLEAR THAT **INBREEDING** HAD BECOME A PROBLEM...

I WANNA NUKE **FLORIDA**!

SIGH...WE'LL LAUNCH THE MISSILES IMMEDIATELY, SIR.

Panel 5: AFTER THE SECOND CIVIL WAR, TERRORISTS ENGINEERED A MYSTERIOUS STERILITY-INDUCING RETROVIRUS WHICH ONLY AFFECTED THE **BUSHES**... FORCING GOVERNMENT SCIENTISTS TO EXPERIMENT WITH **ACCELERATED CLONING TECHNIQUES**...

ER--I THINK WE MAY HAVE A PROBLEM WITH MOLECULAR COHESION.

CAN SOMEBODY GET A **MOP**?

URK.

Panel 6: HAPPILY, A HOLOGRAPHIC SIMULATION OF ONE OF THE **EARLIEST** BUSH PRESIDENTS WAS RECENTLY PERFECTED... AND HISTORIANS SAY HE'S **JUST LIKE THE ORIGINAL**!

SIR, THIS IS A CRISIS--WE'VE GOT FOOD RIOTS IN OLD NEW YORK--AND MUTANT REBELS NOW CONTROL THE CALIFORNIA DMZ!

SOUNDS LIKE WE NEED A **TAX CUT**!

YES, I THOUGHT YOU MIGHT SAY THAT.

TOM TOMORROW©2003

THIS MODERN WORLD

by TOM TOMORROW

AT LAST, THEY CAN BE REVEALED:

GEORGE BUSH'S TOP FIVE SOURCES OF PRE-WAR INTELLIGENCE

1. HIS *OUIJA BOARD.*

THERE YOU HAVE IT, SIR, THE SPIRITS SAY THAT SADDAM *DEFINITELY* POSES AN *IMMINENT THREAT!*

YOU SURE *YOU'RE* NOT MOVIN' THAT POINTER THING AROUND, PAUL?

HEAVEN *FORFEND,* SIR.

2. HIS *DAILY HOROSCOPE.*

CANCER (June 22-July 22): Go on and resolve that unfinished family business--but don't forget your friends in the process!

OKAY, PUT THE TROOPS ON *ALERT*--AND GET THOSE *RECONSTRUCTION CONTRACTS* HANDED OUT!

I'LL CALL HALLIBURTON!

3. *FORTUNE COOKIES.*

Your talents will be recognized and suitably rewarded.

LOOK AT THIS, FELLAS! SUCCESS IS *GUARANTEED!*

THAT WOULD CERTAINLY BE *MY* INTERPRETATION!

UH--YES! MINE TOO!

4. *SUPERMARKET TABLOIDS.*

HEY, CONDI--WHY DIDN'T THE CIA TELL US ABOUT *THIS?*

THEY'RE, UM, TOO BUSY POLITICIZING THE INTELLIGENCE, SIR.

WEEKLY WORLD NEWS

BIGFOOT DIVORCES ELVIS!

SADDAM BUYS WMD'S FROM SPACE ALIENS!

HILLARY BROKERS THE DEAL!

BILL HAS SEX WITH ALIEN!

5. AND, OF COURSE--HIS *MAGIC EIGHT BALL.*

WILL WE FIND A PROVABLE LINK BETWEEN AL QAEDA AND IRAQ?

MY SOURCES SAY YES

I *KNEW* IT!

THIS MODERN WORLD

by TOM TOMORROW

Panel 1: WHEN A FAMOUS ACTOR ENTERS THE POLITICAL FRAY, ALL BETS ARE OFF, AND SO, ONE CANDIDATE NOW *DOMINATES* THE CALIFORNIA RECALL RACE--

--FORMER CHILD STAR *GARY COLEMAN!*

Panel 2: OTHER NEWS STORIES ARE VIRTUALLY *IGNORED* AS THE MEDIA FOCUS OBSESSIVELY ON THE COLEMAN CANDIDACY!

IN IRAQ TODAY, SOME SOLDIERS DIED OR SOMETHING.

IN MORE *IMPORTANT* NEWS, GARY COLEMAN WAVED AT REPORTERS TODAY FROM THE BACK OF HIS *CAMPAIGN LIMO!*

Action McNews

Action McNews

Panel 3: AND OF COURSE, THE *PUNDITS* CAN'T RESIST SLY REFERENCES TO GARY'S *CINEMATIC LEGACY!*

DOES "THE KID FROM LEFT FIELD" HAVE A *CHANCE?* IS HE "ON THE RIGHT *TRACK*"?

AND WILL CALIFORNIANS CHOOSE "GARY COLEMAN-- FOR *SAFETY'S SAKE*"?

*ALL ACTUAL GARY COLEMAN MOVIE TITLES-- BUT YOU KNEW THAT!

Panel 4: INEVITABLE COMPARISONS ARE MADE TO *ANOTHER* ACTOR-TURNED-POLITICIAN!

PRESIDENT REAGAN WAS *MARRIED* TO NANCY REAGAN--AND GARY COLEMAN ONCE *MET* NANCY REAGAN! COINCIDENCE--OR *DESTINY?*

The Next Gipper?

Panel 5: SURE, HIS DETRACTORS DERIDE HIS LACK OF *EXPERIENCE*--BUT ALL THOSE YEARS IN THE PUBLIC EYE HAVE TAUGHT HIM A THING OR TWO ABOUT HANDLING THE *CRITICS!*

I AM *UNIQUELY* QUALIFIED TO HANDLE CALIFORNIA'S BUDGET CRISIS-- HAVING DECLARED BANKRUPTCY *MYSELF* IN 1999!

THE FIRST THING WE'LL DO TO RAISE REVENUE IS AUCTION OFF ANOTHER DATE WITH *ME!*

COLEMAN FOR GOVERNOR

Panel 6: BUT WILL HIS CHARISMA AND FAME BE ENOUGH TO SWAY THE VOTERS OF CALIFORNIA? STAY *TUNED!*

YES, MR. COLEMAN IS A WORLD-FAMOUS ACTOR--BUT DOES THAT *REALLY* QUALIFY HIM TO BE THE *LEADER* OF THIS GREAT STATE?

WELL, ALL I CAN SAY IS-- *WHATCHOO TALKIN' ABOUT*, GRAY DAVIS?

HEH, HEH! DON'T TELL ME YOU DIDN'T SEE *THAT* ONE COMING...

TOM TOMORROW ©2003

THIS MODERN WORLD

by TOM TOMORROW

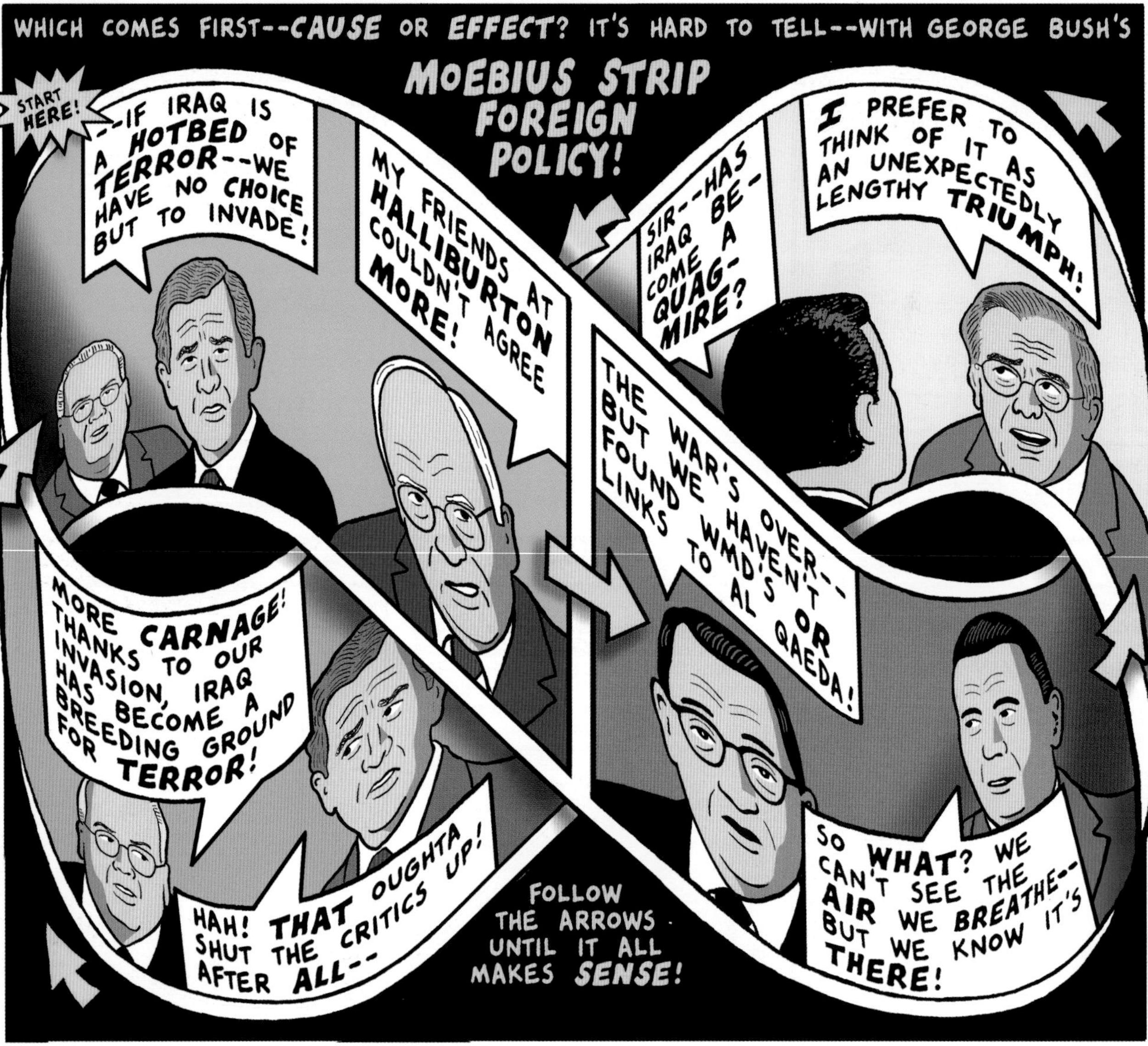
WHICH COMES FIRST--CAUSE OR EFFECT? IT'S HARD TO TELL--WITH GEORGE BUSH'S
MOEBIUS STRIP FOREIGN POLICY!
START HERE!
--IF IRAQ IS A HOTBED OF TERROR--WE HAVE NO CHOICE BUT TO INVADE!
MY FRIENDS AT HALLIBURTON COULDN'T AGREE MORE!
THE WAR'S OVER--BUT WE HAVEN'T FOUND WMD'S OR LINKS TO AL QAEDA!
SO WHAT? WE CAN'T SEE THE AIR WE BREATHE--BUT WE KNOW IT'S THERE!
SIR--HAS IRAQ BECOME A QUAGMIRE?
I PREFER TO THINK OF IT AS AN UNEXPECTEDLY LENGTHY TRIUMPH!
MORE CARNAGE! THANKS TO OUR INVASION, IRAQ HAS BECOME A BREEDING GROUND FOR TERROR!
HAH! THAT OUGHTA SHUT THE CRITICS UP! AFTER ALL--
FOLLOW THE ARROWS UNTIL IT ALL MAKES SENSE!
TOM TOMORROW©2003

THIS MODERN WORLD

by TOM TOMORROW

Panel 1:

THIS WEEK: A **SNEAK PREVIEW** OF AN UPCOMING **BUSH CAMPAIGN AD!**

THE AXIS OF INNUENDO:
TERROR AND THE DEMOCRATS!

Panel 2:

THE **OVERWHELMING SUCCESSES** OF IRAQ AND AFGHANISTAN HAVE CONVINCED THE TERRORISTS THAT **GEORGE W. BUSH MEANS BUSINESS!**

NOT TO **MENTION** THE STEADFAST DETERMINATION WITH WHICH HE HAS PURSUED **TAX CUTS** FOR HIS COUNTRY'S **WEALTHIEST CITIZENS!**

HOW CAN WE EVEN **HOPE** TO PREVAIL AGAINST A MAN OF SUCH STEELY RESOLVE?

Panel 3:

HOWEVER--IF WE DON'T **STAY THE COURSE**, THE EVILDOERS WILL SEE US AS **UNCERTAIN** AND **INDECISIVE!**

THE AMERICANS **MAY** ELECT A **DEMOCRAT** IN 2004!

THEN THE PATHETIC FOOLS WILL BE AT OUR **MERCY!**

Panel 4:

IN FACT--AS THIS DRAMATIZATION CONCLUSIVELY DEMONSTRATES-- IT'S **POSSIBLE** THAT THE TERRORISTS ARE EVEN **CONTRIBUTING** TO DEMOCRATIC COFFERS!

ANOTHER GENEROUS DONATION FROM **AL QAEDA**, SIR!

EX-CELLENT! LARGE, UNMARKED BILLS, AS USUAL?

D.N.C
"We hate America!"

LEGAL DISCLAIMER: ACTUAL CONSPIRACY BETWEEN DEMOCRATIC CANDIDATE AND THOSE WHO SEEK TO DESTROY OUR VERY WAY OF LIFE HAS NOT YET BEEN PROVEN.

Panel 5:

ONE THING'S FOR SURE--WHEN YOU STEP INTO THAT VOTING BOOTH A LITTLE OVER A YEAR FROM NOW, YOUR CHOICE SHOULD BE **CRYSTAL CLEAR!**

☐ **GEORGE W. BUSH** Republican

☐ **A. TERRORIST DUPE** Democrat

Panel 6:

SO REMEMBER--IF YOU **DON'T** VOTE REPUBLICAN IN 2004--

--THEN THE **TERRORISTS** HAVE **ALREADY WON!!**

HOW'D I DO, KARL?

VERY PERSUASIVE, SIR.

PAID FOR BY THE COMMITTEE THAT THINKS YOU'RE STUPID ENOUGH TO RE-ELECT THIS GUY.

TOM TOMORROW©2003

THIS MODERN WORLD

by TOM TOMORROW

CLEAR-EYED CONSERVATIVE REALISTS

CLEAR-EYED CONSERVATIVE REALISTS THOUGHT WE'D BE OUT OF IRAQ IN SIX MONTHS, TOPS.

THE ONLY PROBLEM WE'LL HAVE IS CLEANING UP ALL THE ROSE PETALS THROWN AT OUR TROOPS BY *GRATEFUL IRAQIS!*

INDEED!

CLEAR-EYED CONSERVATIVE REALISTS CONTINUE TO INSIST THAT SADDAM WAS BEHIND THE 9/11 ATTACKS.

THAT'S RIGHT! AND WE DON'T NEED ANY DAMN *EVIDENCE,* EITHER!

EVIDENCE IS FOR *SISSIES!*

CLEAR-EYED CONSERVATIVE REALISTS SEE NO CONTRADICTION IN REQUESTING ANOTHER $87 BILLION FOR IRAQ WHILE PUSHING FOR $107.8 BILLION IN TAX CUTS.

THANK GOD THOSE IRRESPONSIBLE TAX-AND-SPEND *LIBERALS* AREN'T IN CHARGE!

THEN WE'D *REALLY* BE IN TROUBLE!

CLEAR-EYED CONSERVATIVE REALISTS THINK THE MOUNTING DEATH TOLL IN IRAQ PROVES THAT THINGS ARE ACTUALLY GOING REALLY, REALLY WELL.

IF THE TERRORISTS ARE BUSY KILLING OUR SOLDIERS *THERE,* THEY CAN'T COME AFTER US *HERE!*

UNLESS THEY'RE EMBOLDENED BY THE ADMINISTRATION'S *CRITICS,* OF COURSE.

CLEAR-EYED CONSERVATIVE REALISTS WILL PRETTY MUCH BELIEVE ANYTHING THEY'RE TOLD.

THE PRESIDENT SAYS THE TOOTH FAIRY IS *REAL*--AND WORKING WITH *AL QAEDA!*

WELL THEN-- WE'D BETTER BOMB *TOOTH FAIRY LAND!*

I'M GOING TO POST A SCATHING DENUNCIATION OF THE TOOTH FAIRY ON MY *BLOG!*

TOM TOMORROW©2003

THIS MODERN WORLD

by TOM TOMORROW

Panel 1:

COMING SOON: THE UNBIASED, NON-PARTISAN *SEQUEL* TO SHOWTIME'S 9/11 DOCUDRAMA:

THE ABSOLUTELY TRUE STORY OF GEORGE W. BUSH AND THE WAR IN IRAQ!

A KARL ROVE PRODUCTION

STARRING A GUY WHO LOOKS SORT OF LIKE THE PRESIDENT

CO-STARRING SOME ACTORS WHO VAGUELY RESEMBLE MEMBERS OF THE ADMINISTRATION

Panel 2:

YOU'LL *MARVEL* AT THE PRESCIENCE OF GEORGE BUSH'S ADDRESS TO THE NATION ON THE EVE OF WAR!

OUR INVOLVEMENT IN IRAQ WILL LAST *YEARS*--AND COST *HUNDREDS OF BILLIONS OF DOLLARS!*

SO DON'T SAY I DIDN'T *WARN* YOU!

Panel 3:

YOU'LL *CHEER* AS PRESIDENT BUSH PERSONALLY PULLS DOWN A STATUE OF SADDAM--WITH HIS *TEETH!*

THE GRAVEN IMAGES OF TOTALITARIANISM ARE NO MATCH FOR THE *MOLARS* OF *FREE MEN!*

Panel 4:

YOU'LL BE ON THE *EDGE OF YOUR SEAT* DURING THE PRESIDENT'S PREVIOUSLY UNREPORTED *DOGFIGHT* WITH *AL QAEDA OPERATIVES* ON THE WAY TO THE ABRAHAM LINCOLN!

YOU *GOT* 'EM, SIR! WAIT 'TIL THE MEDIA HEAR ABOUT *THIS!*

BLAM!

YOU KEEP QUIET ABOUT THIS, SON! I DON'T WANT TO TURN THIS FLIGHT INTO SOME SORT OF *CHEAP PUBLICITY STUNT!*

Panel 5:

YOU'LL *GASP* AT THE CUNNING OF HIS POSTWAR ANTI-TERROR STRATEGY!

YOU SEE, DICK, AL QAEDA HAS INFILTRATED THE HIGHEST LEVELS OF *CORPORATE AMERICA!*

THESE TAX CUTS AND NO-BID RECONSTRUCTION CONTRACTS ARE ALL PART OF MY PLAN TO LULL THEM INTO A *FALSE SENSE* OF *COMPLACENCY!*

TRULY BRILLIANT, SIR.

Panel 6:

AND YOU'LL BE *STUNNED* BY THE FILM'S MOST *SHOCKING REVELATION!*

SIR, WE HAVE *PROOF* THAT *HILLARY CLINTON* WAS ACTUALLY THE *TWENTIETH HIJACKER*--BUT THE LIBERAL MEDIA REFUSE TO REPORT THE STORY!

DON'T WORRY, DON--SOMEDAY A *CABLE TV DOCUDRAMA* WILL SET THE RECORD *STRAIGHT!*

NOW "LET'S ROLL"--TO *LUNCH!*

YES, SIR.

TOM TOMORROW©2003

THIS MODERN WORLD

by TOM TOMORROW

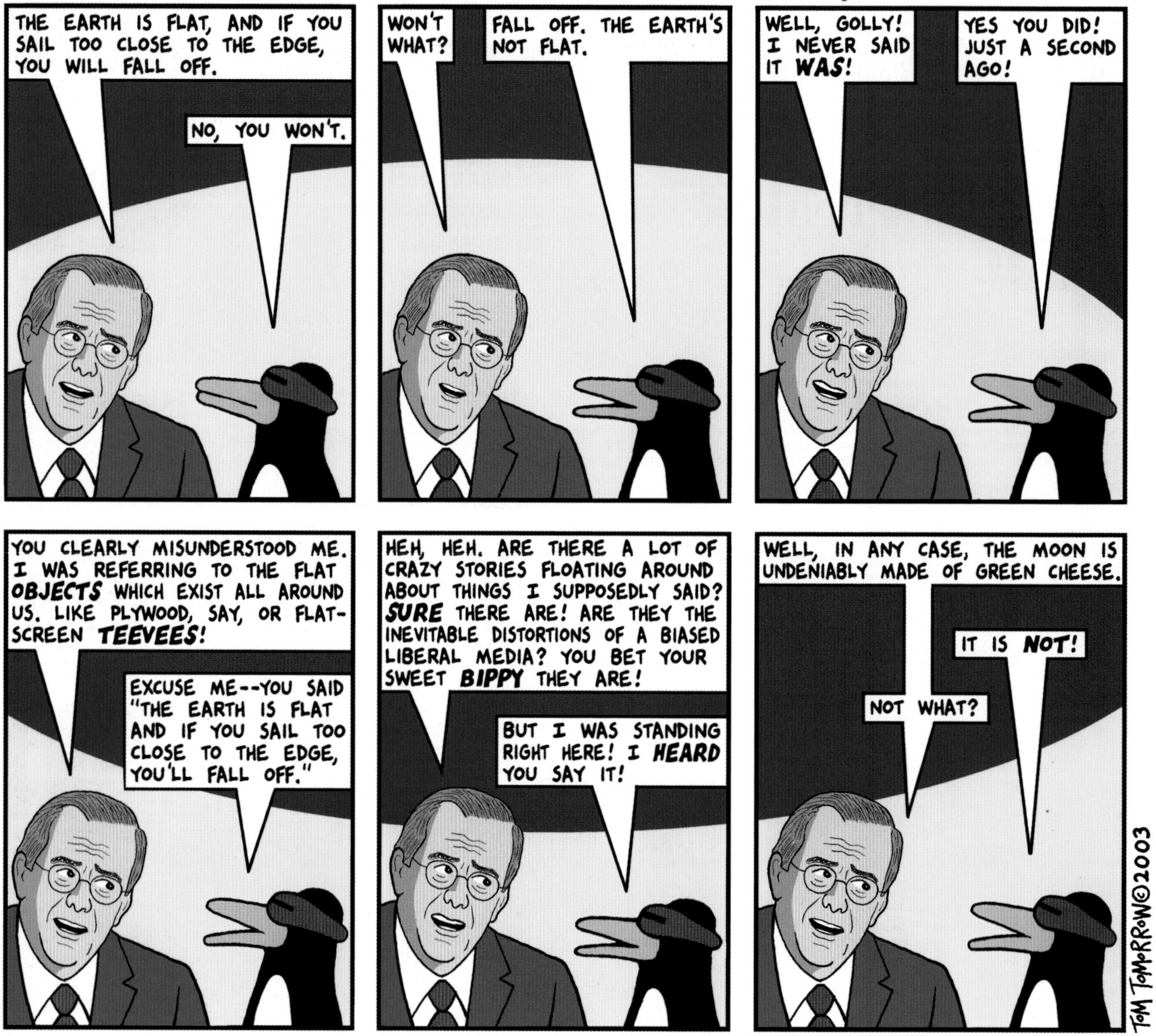

THE EARTH IS FLAT, AND IF YOU SAIL TOO CLOSE TO THE EDGE, YOU WILL FALL OFF.
NO, YOU WON'T.
WON'T WHAT?
FALL OFF. THE EARTH'S NOT FLAT.
WELL, GOLLY! I NEVER SAID IT **WAS**!
YES YOU DID! JUST A SECOND AGO!
YOU CLEARLY MISUNDERSTOOD ME. I WAS REFERRING TO THE FLAT **OBJECTS** WHICH EXIST ALL AROUND US. LIKE PLYWOOD, SAY, OR FLAT-SCREEN **TEEVEES**!
EXCUSE ME--YOU SAID "THE EARTH IS FLAT AND IF YOU SAIL TOO CLOSE TO THE EDGE, YOU'LL FALL OFF."
HEH, HEH. ARE THERE A LOT OF CRAZY STORIES FLOATING AROUND ABOUT THINGS I SUPPOSEDLY SAID? **SURE** THERE ARE! ARE THEY THE INEVITABLE DISTORTIONS OF A BIASED LIBERAL MEDIA? YOU BET YOUR SWEET **BIPPY** THEY ARE!
BUT I WAS STANDING RIGHT HERE! I **HEARD** YOU SAY IT!
WELL, IN ANY CASE, THE MOON IS UNDENIABLY MADE OF GREEN CHEESE.
IT IS **NOT**!
NOT WHAT?
TOM TOMORROW©2003

THIS MODERN WORLD

by TOM TOMORROW

ON THE EVE OF WAR, THE PRESIDENT MAKES A *STARTLING ALLEGATION!*

--AND SO YOU SEE, SADDAM IS SECRETLY CONSPIRING WITH SUCH SUPERVILLAINS AS *CATWOMAN* AND THE *JOKER!*

WE CANNOT WAIT FOR THE SMOKING GUN TO COME IN THE FORM OF A *CLOUD* OF *LAUGHING GAS!*

UNFORTUNATELY, THE STORY IS DISCREDITED AFTER *BATMAN* RETURNS FROM A FACT-FINDING MISSION!

CITIZENS OF GOTHAM CITY, IT IS MY DUTY TO INFORM YOU THAT CATWOMAN AND THE JOKER ARE IN FACT SAFELY INCARCERATED IN *GOTHAM STATE PENITENTIARY!*

HOLY FALSE RATIONALE FOR *WAR*, BATMAN!

SHORTLY THEREAFTER, A COLUMNIST GOES PUBLIC WITH A *MOMENTOUS REVELATION!*

SENIOR OFFICIALS HAVE INFORMED ME THAT *BATMAN* IS REALLY MILLIONAIRE *BRUCE WAYNE!* AND YOU HAVE TO ASK--HOW MUCH CREDIBILITY DOES A MILLIONAIRE PLAYBOY REALLY *HAVE?*

BATMAN! YOUR COVER'S *BLOWN!*

FAITH AND BEGORRAH!

CLOSED CIRCUIT TV

A NATIONAL *FUROR* ENSUES!

THIS LEAK HAS *DESTROYED* BATMAN'S EFFECTIVENESS AS A CRIME FIGHTER!

NONSENSE! HE WAS NEVER REALLY A CRIME *FIGHTER*-- HE WAS MORE OF A CRIME *ANALYST!*

THE WHOLE STORY IS MUCH TOO COMPLICATED. I SUGGEST WE *IGNORE* IT.

BATMAN HOLDS A *PRESS CONFERENCE!*

WHO'S RESPONSIBLE FOR THIS LEAK, BATMAN? THE *RIDDLER?* THE *MAD HATTER?* MR. *FREEZE?*

WELL, CITIZENS--LET'S JUST SAY THAT I HOPE TO SEE *KARL ROVE* FROGMARCHED OUT OF THE WHITE HOUSE--

--IN *BAT-CUFFS!*

AND FINALLY, THE JUSTICE DEPARTMENT IS FORCED TO LAUNCH AN *INVESTIGATION!*

THIS MATTER WILL BE HANDLED BY NON-PARTISAN *CAREER BUREAUCRATS*--LIKE *MR. PENGUIN* HERE!

WE'LL GET TO THE BOTTOM OF THIS--RIGHT, BOYS?

YOU BET, BOSS!

STAY TUNED! THE WILDEST IS *YET TO COME!*

TOM TOMORROW ©2003

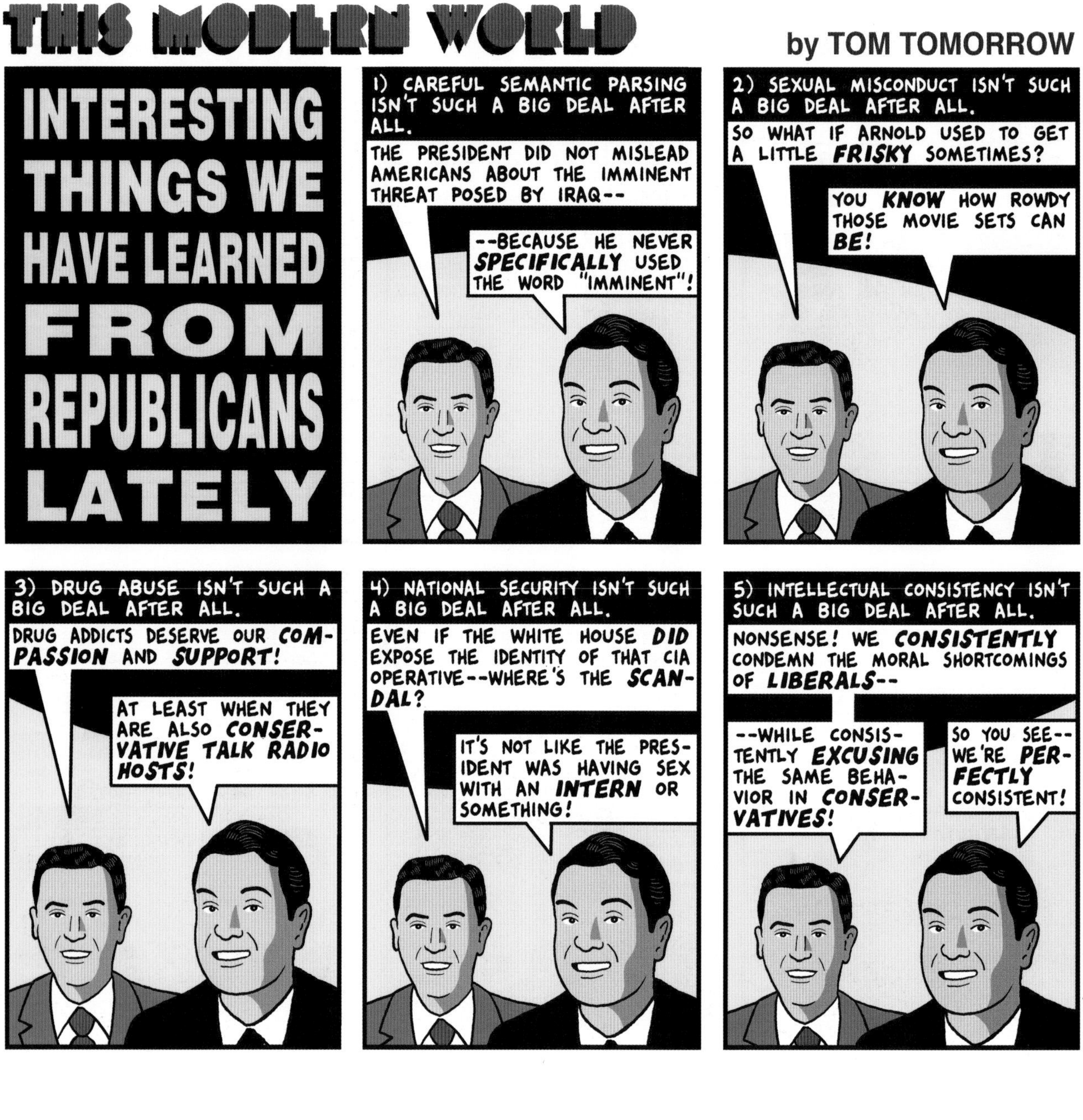
THIS MODERN WORLD
by TOM TOMORROW
INTERESTING THINGS WE HAVE LEARNED FROM REPUBLICANS LATELY
1) CAREFUL SEMANTIC PARSING ISN'T SUCH A BIG DEAL AFTER ALL.
THE PRESIDENT DID NOT MISLEAD AMERICANS ABOUT THE IMMINENT THREAT POSED BY IRAQ--
--BECAUSE HE NEVER SPECIFICALLY USED THE WORD "IMMINENT"!
2) SEXUAL MISCONDUCT ISN'T SUCH A BIG DEAL AFTER ALL.
SO WHAT IF ARNOLD USED TO GET A LITTLE FRISKY SOMETIMES?
YOU KNOW HOW ROWDY THOSE MOVIE SETS CAN BE!
3) DRUG ABUSE ISN'T SUCH A BIG DEAL AFTER ALL.
DRUG ADDICTS DESERVE OUR COMPASSION AND SUPPORT!
AT LEAST WHEN THEY ARE ALSO CONSERVATIVE TALK RADIO HOSTS!
4) NATIONAL SECURITY ISN'T SUCH A BIG DEAL AFTER ALL.
EVEN IF THE WHITE HOUSE DID EXPOSE THE IDENTITY OF THAT CIA OPERATIVE--WHERE'S THE SCANDAL?
IT'S NOT LIKE THE PRESIDENT WAS HAVING SEX WITH AN INTERN OR SOMETHING!
5) INTELLECTUAL CONSISTENCY ISN'T SUCH A BIG DEAL AFTER ALL.
NONSENSE! WE CONSISTENTLY CONDEMN THE MORAL SHORTCOMINGS OF LIBERALS--
--WHILE CONSISTENTLY EXCUSING THE SAME BEHAVIOR IN CONSERVATIVES!
SO YOU SEE--WE'RE PERFECTLY CONSISTENT!
TOM TOMORROW©2003

THIS MODERN WORLD

by TOM TOMORROW

57

THIS MODERN WORLD

by TOM TOMORROW

IT'S THE ZANIEST SITCOM ON TV!

PRESIDENT BABY!

ACCORDING TO THIS PREVIOUSLY UNNOTICED CLAUSE IN THE CONSTITUTION, IT'S **PERFECTLY LEGAL** FOR A SIX-MONTH-OLD TO BE **PRESIDENT!**

I SENSE **WACKY HIJINKS** AHEAD!

PRESIDENT BABY HAS THREE BASIC MOODS: VERY **HAPPY**...

DOES PRESIDENT BABY **LIKE** THE PRIME MINISTER? YES HE **DOES!** HE'S SUCH A NICE **COOPERATIVE** PRIME MINISTER, YES HE **IS!**

GURGLE!

...VERY **SAD**...

DON'T WORRY, PRESIDENT BABY! YOU CAN HAVE YOUR WAR--NO MATTER **WHAT** THE FRENCH SAY!

WAAAAAAH!

...AND VERY **CONFUSED!**

SIR, WERE YOUR WAR PLANS BASED ON **BAD INTELLIGENCE** AND **FLAWED ASSUMPTIONS?**

PRESIDENT BABY HAS NO IDEA WHAT YOU'RE TALKING ABOUT.

PLEASE GO NOW.

MEANWHILE, PRESIDENT BABY'S **GRADE SCHOOL ADMINISTRATION** TAKES CARE OF THE DAY-TO-DAY **DETAILS!**

THE TERRORIST ATTACKS WERE ALL THAT DUMB OL' **BILL CLINTON'S** FAULT!

AND THINGS ARE GOIN' **GREAT** IN IRAQ! 'CAUSE WE **SAY** SO!

WE'RE **RUBBER** AND THE DEMOCRATS ARE **GLUE!** SO **THERE!**

NYAH NYAH **NYAH!**

Librʋls aRe PoopY Heads

HaNNiTY RULEZ

Tom ToMoRRoW ©2003

58

THIS MODERN WORLD

by TOM TOMORROW

CHICKEN HAWK DOWN

WHILE OTHERS RISKED THEIR LIVES IN IRAQ AND AFGHANISTAN, *HE* FOUGHT BRAVELY ON THE BATTLEFIELD OF THE *INTERNET!*

I'M WAGING WAR ON THE ISLAMO-FASCISTS--ON MY *BLOG!*

EACH DAY HE SURFED THE WEB WITH *STEADFAST RESOLVE!*

THIS WALL STREET JOURNAL EDITORIAL *PROVES* THAT CRITICS OF THE ADMINISTRATION ARE OBJECTIVELY *PRO-TERROR!*

I SHALL LINK TO IT *IMMEDIATELY*--IN THE NAME OF *FREEDOM!*

HE MAY NOT HAVE BEEN DODGING BULLETS--BUT HE *DID* RECEIVE THE OCCASIONAL *NASTY EMAIL!*

Hey moron, if you think the war is such a good idea, why don't you enlist??

YIKES--*IN-COMING!*

BUT THEN ONE DAY, THIS COURAGEOUS ARMCHAIR WARRIOR WAS FELLED WITHOUT WARNING--BY *CARPAL TUNNEL SYNDROME!*

AAUUGH! MY *WRIST!*

MEDIC!!

SHAKEN BY THE LOSS, HIS COMRADES NONETHELESS SOLDIERED ON WITHOUT HIM.

DAMMIT! WE LOST ANOTHER GOOD MAN!

WAR IS *HELL!!*

HEY MA--ARE WE OUTTA *CHEETOS?*

TOM TOMORROW©2003

THIS MODERN WORLD

by TOM TOMORROW

THE NEW LITERALISTS

IT'S THE DEBATE TACTIC THAT'S SWEEPING THE NATION!

NOTHING'S QUITE AS PERSUASIVE AS SEMANTIC QUIBBLING!

SURE, THE PRESIDENT SAID SADDAM POSED AN "URGENT" AND "GATHERING" THREAT--AND THAT HE WAS CAPABLE OF LAUNCHING A CHEMICAL OR BIOLOGICAL ATTACK WITHIN FORTY-FIVE MINUTES--

--BUT HE NEVER LITERALLY USED THE WORD "IMMINENT"!

AND HE MAY HAVE GIVEN A SPEECH IN FRONT OF A GIANT "MISSION ACCOMPLISHED" BANNER--BUT THAT PROVES NOTHING--

--BECAUSE HE DID NOT LITERALLY HANG THE BANNER HIMSELF!

AND WHILE IRAQ MAY BE A GROWING QUAGMIRE WITH NO LIGHT AT THE END OF THE TUNNEL, IT IS NOT LITERALLY ANOTHER VIETNAM!

YOU SEE, IRAQ IS IN THE MIDDLE EAST-- NOT SOUTHEAST ASIA!

OH--AND ONE MORE THING--

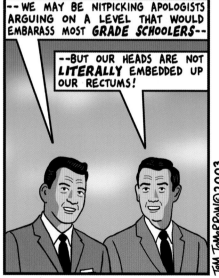

-- WE MAY BE NITPICKING APOLOGISTS ARGUING ON A LEVEL THAT WOULD EMBARASS MOST GRADE SCHOOLERS--

--BUT OUR HEADS ARE NOT LITERALLY EMBEDDED UP OUR RECTUMS!

TOM TOMORROW©2003

60

THIS MODERN WORLD

by TOM TOMORROW

RIPPED FROM THE FRONT PAGES OF TODAY'S NEWSPAPERS--

THE HOMO-SEXUAL MENACE

SURE, POP CULTURE PRESENTS THEM AS *HARMLESS* AND *ADORABLE*...

THOSE GAY GUYS ON THAT TV SHOW ARE *HILARIOUS*!

IF ONLY THERE WERE *MORE* HOMOSEXUALS IN THE ENTERTAINMENT INDUSTRY!

AND SINCE MANY AMERICANS PRIDE THEMSELVES ON THEIR *TOLERANCE*, GAY *MARRIAGE* SEEMS INCREASINGLY *PLAUSIBLE*...

WE JUST WANT THE RIGHT TO AFFIRM OUR COMMITMENT TO EACH OTHER-- LIKE ANY *STRAIGHT* COUPLE!

WELL, I DON'T *LIKE* IT--BUT I GUESS I CAN *TOLERATE* IT...

BUT *DON'T BE FOOLED!* THE HOMOSEXUALS HAVE A *SINISTER AGENDA*--AND THEY'LL DO *ANYTHING* TO ACHIEVE IT!

PSSST! OPERATION *SUBVERT HETEROSEXUALITY* IS PROCEEDING ACCORDING TO PLAN!

I'LL INFORM H.Q. *IMMEDIATELY*!

BUS STOP

IF THEY'RE ALLOWED TO UNDERMINE THE SACRED INSTITUTION OF *MARRIAGE*--THERE'S NO *TELLING* WHAT COULD HAPPEN *NEXT*!

THE *HECK* WITH MY TRADITIONAL HETEROSEXUAL LIFESTYLE! *I'M* MARRYING A GOAT!

I'M HAVING NON-PROCREATIVE SEX WITH THE ENTIRE CITY OF *TOPEKA, KANSAS*!

SO STAY *VIGILANT*, CITIZENS--AND *BEWARE* THE *HOMOSEXUAL MENACE*!

YOU KNOW, I'M NOT *REALLY* SURE GAY MARRIAGE WOULD LEAD INEVITABLY TO WIDESPREAD SEX WITH ANIMALS...

WELL, YOU'RE NOT EXACTLY AN IMPARTIAL OBSERVER HERE, ARE YOU?

TOM TOMORROW©2003

THIS MODERN WORLD

by TOM TOMORROW

LIFE IN THE BUBBLE

DON'T YOU WORRY YOUR PRETTY LITTLE HEAD ABOUT A *THING*!

HE DOESN'T READ NEWSPAPERS.

"THE BEST WAY TO GET THE NEWS IS FROM OBJECTIVE SOURCES...AND THE MOST OBJECTIVE SOURCES *I* HAVE ARE PEOPLE ON MY STAFF WHO TELL ME WHAT'S HAPPENING IN THE WORLD!"*

HEH, HEH.

FAIR AND BALANCED, THAT'S US!

*ACTUAL QUOTE.

HE NEVER SEES A PROTESTER.

SORRY, PAL--THE "FREE SPEECH ZONE" IS OVER *THERE*--OUT OF SIGHT BEHIND THAT LARGE *BARRICADE!*

MY MISTAKE-- I THOUGHT THE ENTIRE *COUNTRY* WAS A "FREE SPEECH ZONE."

BUSH IS A WANKER!

HE DOESN'T ATTEND THE FUNERALS OF SOLDIERS KILLED IN IRAQ.

UM--THE PRESIDENT HAS BEEN-- ER--*BUSY.*

VERY, VERY *BUSY.*

YES, INDEEDY.

I HAVE TO GO NOW.

EVEN A PLANNED SPEECH TO THE BRITISH PARLIAMENT WAS CANCELLED TO AVOID HECKLERS.

THOSE ANTI-WAR MP'S CAN BE *SO* IMPOLITE!

THEY'RE NOWHERE *NEAR* AS DOCILE AS OUR *DEMOCRATS!*

KIND OF EXPLAINS A LOT, DOESN'T IT?

THE WAR'S GOING *GREAT*, GEORGE! NOW YOU STAY IN THERE AND BEHAVE AND MAYBE WE'LL LET YOU WEAR THE *FLIGHT SUIT* AGAIN!

ISN'T HE *ADORABLE?* YOU CAN SIT HIM IN FRONT OF "TELETUBBIES" AND HE'S GOOD FOR *HOURS!*

OH OH!

TOM TOMORROW©2003

THIS MODERN WORLD

by TOM TOMORROW

ZEN MASTER GEORGE JUNIOR

ANOTHER CARTOON SEQUEL TWELVE YEARS IN THE MAKING!

SEE THE ORIGINAL: www.thismodernworld.com/zen.jpg

THE BEST WAY TO PROTECT SENIORS--

--IS TO UNDERMINE THE STABILITY OF MEDICARE!

TO ENSURE A CLEAN ENVIRONMENT--

--WE MUST WEAKEN ENVIRONMENTAL REGULATIONS!

I'VE MADE THE WORLD A MORE PEACEFUL PLACE--

--BY WAGING A UNILATERAL, PRE-EMPTIVE WAR!

THE WORSE THINGS GET IN IRAQ--

--THE CLOSER WE ARE TO VICTORY!

AND THE MOST IMPORTANT LESSON OF ALL--

THE FAILURES OF THIS ADMINISTRATION--

--CAN ONLY BE BLAMED ON OUR CRITICS!

TOM TOMORROW ©2003

THIS MODERN WORLD

by TOM TOMORROW

Panel 1: ONCE AGAIN, IT'S TIME TO CHECK IN ON...
PARALLEL EARTH!

AS YOU KNOW, A QUIRK IN THEIR ELECTION LAWS LED OUR INTER-DIMENSIONAL COUNTERPARTS TO ELECT A **SMALL CUTE DOG** AS **THEIR** PRESIDENT THREE YEARS AGO...

ARF!

Panel 2: NOW, AFTER SEVERAL YEARS OF CONSTANT **CRISIS**, SUPPORT FOR THE SMALL CUTE DOG IS BEGINNING TO **FRAY**...

ISN'T IT KIND OF WEIRD HOW THEY NEVER LET HIM SPEAK FOR **HIMSELF**?

I'M STARTING TO WONDER IF HE'S ANYTHING MORE THAN A **FIGUREHEAD**!

Panel 3: AND ADMITTEDLY, THERE HAVE BEEN MISSTEPS...ONE PHOTO OP SEEMS **PARTICULARLY** ILL-CONCEIVED IN RETROSPECT...

MISSION ACCOMPLISHED

ARF!

THUMP THUMP THUMP

Panel 4: AND WITH AN ELECTION ON THE HORIZON, OPPOSITION PARTY CANDIDATES HAVE BEGUN TO OPENLY CHALLENGE THE SMALL CUTE DOG'S LEADERSHIP.

THE SMALL CUTE DOG HAS BEEN POOPING ON THE LAWNS OF OUR ALLIES SINCE THE **DAY HE TOOK OFFICE**!

PARALLEL HOWARD DEAN

Panel 5: ALL IN ALL, IT'S SHAPING UP TO BE ONE OF THE MOST DIVISIVE CAMPAIGNS IN PARALLEL HISTORY.

THE SMALL CUTE DOG COULDN'T LEAD US OUT OF THIS MESS IF THE TRAIL WERE MARKED WITH **FRESH URINE**!

WHAT **IS** IT WITH YOU OPPOSITION PARTY TYPES AND YOUR IRRATIONAL DOG HATRED?

PARALLEL BEARDED GUY

Panel 6: OF COURSE, THE SMALL CUTE DOG HIMSELF IS FAR TOO BUSY TO WORRY ABOUT ALL THE PARTISAN BICKERING.

WHAT IS IT BOY? YOU SAY WE NEED TO STEP THROUGH THE DOOR OF **FURTHER CORPORATE DE-REGULATION**?

I THINK HE JUST WANTS TO GO OUT AND PLAY FETCH.

NOBODY ASKED YOU.

WHINE! ARF! GRRRR!

TOM TOMORROW©2003

THIS MODERN WORLD

by TOM TOMORROW

GENERAL TOMMY FRANKS SAYS THAT IF THERE'S ANOTHER MAJOR TERRORIST ATTACK, IT MAY WELL CAUSE AMERICANS TO QUESTION THE CONSTITUTION AND BEGIN TO "MILITARIZE OUR COUNTRY"--AND *I* THINK HE'S PROBABLY *RIGHT!*

HOLD ON THERE, COWBOY.

YOU THINK *THIS* IS THE WORST CRISIS THIS COUNTRY HAS EVER BEEN THROUGH? WHAT ABOUT THE CIVIL WAR? TWO WORLD WARS? AND THE COLD WAR-- REMEMBER *THAT* ONE? KOREA, VIETNAM, CONSTANT THREAT OF *NUCLEAR ANNIHILATION*?

OUR CONSTITUTION FACED SERIOUS CHALLENGES EACH STEP OF THE WAY--FROM LINCOLN'S SUSPENSION OF HABEAS CORPUS TO THE JAPANESE INTERNMENT CAMPS TO THE COINTEL PROGRAM--BUT IT SURVIVED PRETTY MUCH *INTACT*--

--BUT *NOW*, BECAUSE OF NINETEEN PSYCHOPATHS WITH BOXCUTTERS-- AND THE FEAR OF WHAT THEIR FRIENDS MIGHT DO--YOU'RE READY TO SCRAP OUR SYSTEM OF GOV- ERNMENT *ENTIRELY*, TO TRADE IN DEMOCRACY FOR A *MILITARY GOVERNMENT*--ALL ON THE OFF CHANCE THAT IT'LL KEEP YOU A LITTLE BIT *SAFER*?

ACTUALLY, I'M JUST HOPING TO SEE YOU AND YOUR LIBERAL BUDDIES BEHIND RAZOR WIRE.

YEAH, I FIGURED AS MUCH.

TOM TOMORROW©2003

65

by TOM TOMORROW

EXCUSE US, CITIZEN--WE'RE WITH THE *PATRIOTISM POLICE*.

WE'D LIKE TO ASK YOU A FEW QUESTIONS. STRICTLY ROUTINE.

?

WHEN YOU HEARD ABOUT THE CAPTURE OF SADDAM, WOULD YOU SAY YOU WERE (A) DELIRIOUSLY OVERJOYED, (B) QUIETLY PLEASED, OR (C) BITTERLY DISAPPOINTED IN AN AMERICA-HATING KIND OF WAY?

ER--WELL--GIVEN *THOSE* CHOICES, I GUESS I'D HAVE TO SAY "QUIETLY PLEASED"--I MEAN, IT'S OBVIOUSLY GOOD NEWS--

--BUT I JUST DON'T THINK IT REALLY CHANGES ANYTHING-- WE'RE STILL CAUGHT IN A QUAGMIRE, SOLDIERS ARE STILL DYING, AND--ER--UH--

UH OH.

SIR, WE'RE GOING TO HAVE TO CHARGE YOU WITH "INSUFFICIENT ENTHUSIASM FOR A GLORIOUS VICTORY OF THE HOMELAND."

I'M AFRAID YOU'LL HAVE TO COME WITH US.

WAIT! I *MEANT* TO SAY "DELIRIOUSLY OVERJOYED!"

UH HUH.

TELL IT TO THE JUDGE.

Tom Tomorrow ©2003

THIS MODERN WORLD

by TOM TOMORROW

FAIR AND BALANCED

WELCOME BACK TO THE NETWORK *REAL* AMERICANS TRUST! WE'RE JOINED BY A *LICENSED REPUBLICAN PSYCHIATRIST* TO DISCUSS THE *PRICKLY PROPHET OF PESSIMISM*, DEMOCRATIC FRONTRUNNER *HOWARD DEAN!*

EVERYTHING IS GREAT...PRESIDENT

SO, DOCTOR--WHAT'S *UP* WITH THE *DOUR DOYEN OF DESPAIR*, ANYWAY? WHY CAN'T HE JUST BE *CHEERFUL* AND *UPBEAT*--LIKE *PRESIDENT BUSH?*

IS AN OPTIMIST...WAR IN IRAQ IS A

WELL, I BELIEVE THE *ACRIMONIOUS AMBASSADOR OF ANTIPATHY* IS SUFFERING FROM A CONDITION *I* CALL *CLINICAL AMERICA-HATRED!* TO PUT IT IN LAYMAN'S TERMS, HE *HATES AMERICA!*

I SEE!

SUCCESS...PROSPERITY JUST AROUND

NOW DOCTOR, I REALIZE YOU HAVEN'T PERSONALLY EXAMINED THE *ILL-TEMPERED INTERNUNCIO OF IRRITABILITY*--BUT IS IT *POSSIBLE* THAT HE'S AN EARLY VICTIM OF *MAD COW DISEASE?*

WELL, IT *WOULD* BE IRRESPONSIBLE OF ME TO *SPECULATE*--

THE CORNER...DEMOCRATS BAD,

--BUT HYPOTHETICALLY SPEAKING, IF HE *DID* HAVE MAD COW DISEASE, IT WOULD LITERALLY BE EATING *HOLES* IN HIS *BRAIN*--WHICH *WOULD* SHED LIGHT ON HIS SEEMINGLY INEXPLICABLE BEHAVIOR!

WHETHER OR NOT HE *DOES* HAVE MAD COW DISEASE, HOWEVER--

REPUBLICANS GOOD...YOU ARE

--IT'S CLEAR THAT THE *MALCONTENT MAVEN OF MISERY* BELONGS IN A *NUTHOUSE*--NOT IN THE *WHITE HOUSE!*

SPEAKING AS A LICENSED REPUBLICAN PSYCHIATRIST, OF COURSE.

WELL, THANKS FOR YOUR *PROFESSIONAL INSIGHT*, DOC! WE'LL BE BACK WITH *MORE* FAIR AND BALANCED NEWS--AFTER THESE MESSAGES!

TOM TOMORROW©2004

GETTING SLEEPY...VERY, VERY SLEE

THIS MODERN WORLD

by TOM TOMORROW

REFERENCE SOURCES OF TERROR

THIS IS TRUE: THE FBI IS WARNING POLICE TO WATCH OUT FOR PEOPLE CARRYING *FARMER'S ALMANACS*--WHICH, THEY SAY, COULD BE HELPFUL TO *TERRORISTS*!

WHY, THIS BOOK COULD SUPPLY THEM WITH A ROUGH IDEA OF WHAT THE WEATHER *MIGHT* BE LIKE ON THE DAY OF A PLANNED *ATTACK*!

NOT TO *MENTION* ALL THE HELPFUL *GARDENING TIPS*!

OF COURSE, THERE ARE PLENTY OF *OTHER* BOOKS OUT THERE WHICH TERRORISTS MIGHT *ALSO* FIND USEFUL!

IT'S A DIRECTORY OF *TOURIST LANDMARKS*--AND *SPECIFIC INSTRUCTIONS* FOR *LOCATING* THEM! I CAUGHT 'EM WITH IT--*RED-HANDED*!

WHO *IS* THIS "ARTHUR FROMMER"--AND *WHY* DOES HE *HATE AMERICA*?

AND EVERY DAY, SO-CALLED "NEWSPAPERS" PROVIDE A *TREASURE TROVE* OF POLITICAL, MILITARY AND CULTURAL INFORMATION!

YES, THAT'S RIGHT, OFFICER! HE *PORES* OVER IT EVERY MORNING--*FIRST THING*!

WHO ARE YOU TALKING TO, HONEY?

FOR THAT MATTER, LIBRARIES AND BOOKSTORES ARE *FULL* OF PUBLICATIONS AND PERIODICALS WHICH COULD EASILY BE PUT TO *NEFARIOUS USES*!

THIS THESAURUS WILL *REALLY* HELP ME PUNCH UP MY NEXT CALL TO *JIHAD*!

I'M GOING TO GAIN INSIGHT INTO THE DECADENT WEST BY CAREFULLY STUDYING THIS *SPORTS ILLUSTRATED SWIMSUIT ISSUE*!

SO *BE ALERT*, CITIZENS--BECAUSE A *LITTLE KNOWLEDGE* IS A *DANGEROUS THING*!

EXCUSE ME--WHAT TIME DOES THE TRAIN TO NEW HAVEN LEAVE?

HAH! YOU AND YOUR BUDDIES IN AL QAEDA WOULD *LIKE* TO KNOW--*WOULDN'T YOU*?!

LATE-BREAKING UPDATE: THE FBI HAS JUST LEARNED OF SOMETHING CALLED "THE INTERNET." IF SIGHTED, IT SHOULD BE APPROACHED WITH *EXTREME CAUTION*!

THIS MODERN WORLD

by TOM TOMORROW

KARL ROVE: RENAISSANCE MAN

IT'S A LITTLE KNOWN FACT THAT KARL ROVE HOLDS ADVANCED DEGREES IN A NUMBER OF DISPARATE FIELDS, INCLUDING **ASTROPHYSICS**...

--SO YOU SEE, SIR, A MOON BASE AND A MANNED EXPEDITION TO MARS ARE THE MOST **LOGICAL** EXPENDITURES WE COULD AUTHORIZE! SPEAKING FROM A **STRICTLY SCIENTIFIC VIEWPOINT**, OF COURSE!

CAN I WEAR A **SPACESUIT**? THAT WOULD BE EVEN COOLER THAN A **FLIGHT SUIT**!

...ECONOMICS...

THIS PROPOSED REFORM OF OUR IMMIGRATION POLICY IS CERTAIN TO PROVIDE ECONOMIC STIMULUS IN **SEVERAL** KEY SECTORS!

AND IT'LL HELP ME LOOK **COMPASSIONATE**!

IF YOU SAY SO, SIR. I REALLY DON'T CONCERN MYSELF WITH THE **POLITICAL IMPLICATIONS** OF MY WORK.

...AND **SOCIAL SCIENCES**...JUST TO NAME A **FEW**!

ACCORDING TO MY STATISTICAL ANALYSIS OF CURRENT SOCIOLOGICAL INDICATORS, IT IS IMPERATIVE FOR THIS ADMINISTRATION TO SPEND 1.5 BILLION DOLLARS PROMOTING **TRADITIONAL MARRIAGE**!

HEH! THAT COULD MAKE **GAY MARRIAGE** A MAJOR ISSUE IN THE CAMPAIGN!

AS I SAY, SIR, THAT'S NOT REALLY MY AREA OF EXPERTISE.

KARL ROVE--SELFLESSLY APPLYING HIS PRODIGIOUS TALENTS FOR THE **BETTERMENT** OF **AMERICA**!

SIR--MY LATEST RESEARCH INTO TRENDS AND CONDITIONS SUGGESTS THAT ANOTHER **UPPER INCOME TAX CUT** IS IN ORDER!

ALL RIGHT THEN, KARL! WHATEVER YOU SAY!

ALSO, I BELIEVE SOMEONE SHOULD LEAVE A HORSE'S HEAD IN PAUL O'NEILL'S BED. SPEAKING AS A TRAINED BEHAVIORALIST, OF COURSE.

NO PROBLEMO!

THIS MODERN WORLD

by TOM TOMORROW

Panel 1:
THE NEWS CAME AS A BIT OF A SHOCK AT FIRST.

HERE'S A SURPRISING STORY, BIFF! SCIENTISTS HAVE DISCOVERED THAT OUR WORLD ACTUALLY *IS* A GIANT COMPUTER SIMULATION CONTROLLED BY MALEVOLENT MACHINES--JUST LIKE IN THOSE *MOVIES!*

YOU KNOW WHAT *ELSE* IS SURPRISING, WANDA? THE *WEEKEND WEATHER FORECAST!*

Panel 2:
THE DEMOCRATIC CANDIDATES DIDN'T KNOW HOW TO RESPOND...

WE WERE LIVING IN A COMPUTER SIMULATION *BEFORE* SADDAM WAS CAPTURED--AND WE'RE, UM, STILL LIVING IN ONE *NOW!*

IF HOWARD *DEAN* IS ELECTED, HE'LL PROBABLY END UP--UH--*DELETING* OUR *HARD DRIVE!* OR SOMETHING.

Panel 3:
...BUT THE ADMINISTRATION HAD NO DIFFICULTY SEIZING THE ADVANTAGE.

SO IF YOU *THINK* ABOUT IT, THE WHOLE IRAQ WAR IS JUST A BIG *VIDEO GAME!* WHO'S GOING TO GET UPSET ABOUT A *VIDEO GAME?*

ALSO, IN LIGHT OF THIS NEWS, WE'VE DECIDED TO DRILL *ANWAR*.

IT'S JUST A *SIMULATED* WILDLIFE REFUGE, AFTER ALL!

Panel 4:
PUNDITS TRIED TO PUT IT ALL IN PERSPECTIVE...

HIS CRITICS SAY BUSH HAS NO *SUBSTANCE*--BUT DOESN'T THAT MAKE HIM THE *PERFECT* LEADER FOR A *SIMULATED WORLD?*

ALL *I* WANT TO KNOW IS--DOES THIS MEAN I CAN CHEAT ON MY *DIET* NOW? HA, HA!

HA, HA!

Panel 5:
...WHILE THE VOTING PUBLIC GREW INCREASINGLY APATHETIC.

IT TURNS OUT THAT PRESIDENT BUSH AND KEN LAY HAD *GROUP SEX* WITH OSAMA AND SADDAM RIGHT BEFORE 9/11!

AH, SO WHAT? IT WAS ONLY *SIMULATED* SEX!

Panel 6:
AND THEN GEORGE BUSH DECLARED HIMSELF SUPREME RULER OF THE SIMULATED WORLD.

IT'S WHAT THE MACHINE OVERLORDS *WANT* ME TO DO!

SIR! GREAT NEWS! OUR CALCULATIONS WERE MISTAKEN! WE DON'T LIVE IN A SIMULATION AFTER ALL!

GUARDS! ARREST THIS ENEMY COMBATANT *IMMEDIATELY!* YOUR SUPREME RULER *COMMANDS* IT!

TOM TOMORROW ©2004

THIS MODERN WORLD

by TOM TOMORROW

FALL, 2002...

ALL RIGHT, AGENT SQUIRREL--WE NEED THE *BEST INTEL* YOU CAN *GIVE US* ABOUT SADDAM'S WEAPONS OF MASS DESTRUCTION!

AS LONG AS IT PROVES WHAT WE ALREADY THINK WE KNOW.

YOU CAN COUNT ON ME, SIRS.

LATER...

I GUESS THESE TRACTOR TRAILERS *COULD* BE SOME SORT OF WEAPONS LABS--IF YOU HOLD THE PHOTO JUST RIGHT AND SORT OF *SQUINT*--

THEY LOOK VERY THREATENING TO ME.

STILL LATER...

ACCORDING TO THIS DOCUMENT, SADDAM TRIED TO BUY URANIUM FROM NIGER--BUT IT'S ON THE WRONG LETTERHEAD AND SIGNED BY THE WRONG GUY--

DETAILS, SHMEETAILS! IT'S BETTER THAN *NOTHING!*

FINALLY...

HERE YOU GO, SIRS--IT'S NOT MUCH, BUT IT'S THE BEST WE COULD COME UP WITH--

LOOKS LIKE *PROOF POSITIVE* TO *ME!*

IF OUR DISPASSIONATE INTELLIGENCE ANALYSTS SAY SADDAM HAS WMD'S-- THEN I GUESS WAR IS OUR *ONLY OPTION!*

IT WON'T BE *OUR* FAULT IF THINGS GO BADLY!

UH OH...

WE'RE SIMPLY ACTING ON THE BEST INFORMATION *AVAILABLE!*

TOM TOMORROW©2004...WITH APOLOGIES TO HANNA-BARBERA!

71

THIS MODERN WORLD

by TOM TOMORROW

Panel 1:

IT'S TIME FOR ANOTHER EXCITING EPISODE OF EVERYONE'S FAVORITE CRIME DRAMA--

PARTISAN INVESTIGATIONS UNIT

"If we're not looking into it-- It's not worth looking into!"

THIS WEEK: THE TEAM TRIES TO FIND SOMETHING TO DO.

Panel 2:

BOSS--THEY STILL HAVEN'T FOUND OUT WHO TOLD ROBERT NOVAK THAT VALERIE PLAME WAS A CIA OPERATIVE! YOU WANT *US* TO CHECK IT OUT?

NAH! I'M *SURE* THE MISCREANT WILL STEP FORWARD EVENTUALLY.

SNICKER!

Panel 3:

THE 9/11 COMMISSION SAYS THEY CAN'T FINISH THEIR WORK IN THE TIME ALLOTTED! SHOULD WE SEND SOME PEOPLE OVER TO HELP *OUT*?

HEY--IT'S NOT *MY* PROBLEM IF THEY'RE A BUNCH OF DAMN *PROCRASTINATORS*!

WHAT *ELSE* HAVE WE GOT?

Panel 4:

THE PRESIDENT'S SETTING UP A COMMISSION TO INVESTIGATE PRE-WAR INTELLIGENCE FAILURES! WE *COULD* LEND THEM A HAND!

AHEM! YES, WELL-- WE'LL CERTAINLY PUT AS MUCH EFFORT INTO THAT AS THE PRESIDENT *WANTS* US TO!

WINK!

Panel 5:

BOSS! JANET JACKSON'S NIPPLE WAS *BRIEFLY VISIBLE* DURING THE SUPER BOWL HALFTIME SHOW! THE FCC IS CALLING FOR A *FULL INVESTIGATION*!

A *NIPPLE*? ON *NATIONAL TELEVISION*?!

YES, SIR.

Panel 6:

WELL WHAT THE HELL ARE YOU *WAITING* FOR? GET A *MOVE* ON! THE AMERICAN PEOPLE DESERVE *ANSWERS*!

I'LL COMPILE A LIST OF *WITNESSES*!

I'LL REVIEW THE *TAPE*!

LET'S *ROLL!!*

NEXT: AN INNOCENT *BREAST*--OR A THREAT TO *NATIONAL SECURITY*? THE P.I.U. IS *ON THE CASE*!

TOM TOMORROW ©2004

THIS MODERN WORLD

by TOM TOMORROW

HOW CONSERVATIVES SEE IT

DEMOCRATS WHO DISLIKE THE PRESIDENT ARE **ANGRY** AND **DELUSIONAL**--

HOW CAN THEY **NOT** SUPPORT HIM? HE IS THE **PRESIDENT!**

IT'S NOT LIKE WE'RE TALKING ABOUT **SLICK WILLIE** HERE!

I THINK THEY MUST BE **CLINICALLY INSANE!**

--BUT THE EVANGELICAL CHRISTIANS WHO FORM THE CORE OF BUSH'S **SUPPORT** ARE **PERFECTLY RATIONAL.**

WHEN WE ARE TRANSPORTED BODILY TO HEAVEN DURING THE RAPTURE-- WILL THE FILLINGS IN OUR TEETH BE **LEFT BEHIND?**

I DON'T KNOW--BUT IT IS CERTAINLY A QUESTION WORTH **PONDERING!**

JOHN KERRY DESERVES **CONTEMPT** FOR HIS CRITICISM OF A WAR HE EXPERIENCED **FIRSTHAND**--

HOW DO WE KNOW HE EVEN REALLY **WENT** TO VIETNAM, HUH? ANSWER ME **THAT!**

HE PROBABLY SPENT THE SIXTIES HANGING OUT IN **HOLLYWOOD** WITH **HANOI JANE!**

--BUT QUESTIONS ABOUT GEORGE BUSH'S NATIONAL GUARD RECORD ARE BEYOND THE **PALE.**

THE PRESIDENT **SAYS** HE FULFILLED HIS DUTY! WHAT MORE PROOF DOES ANYONE **NEED?**

THE **IMPORTANT** THING IS, HE **DIDN'T** HANG OUT WITH **HANOI JANE!**

AND OF COURSE, IT'S PERFECTLY ACCEPTABLE FOR **CONSERVATIVE** PUNDITS TO TOSS OUT ALL MANNER OF WILD ACCUSATIONS--

DEMOCRATS **HATE AMERICA!** THEY **WANT** THE TERRORISTS TO WIN! THEY'RE SECRETLY ROOTING FOR THE **TOTAL COLLAPSE** OF **WESTERN CIVILIZATION!**

AND THEY LIKE TO **DROWN KITTENS!**

--BUT GOD FORBID LIBERALS SHOULD EVER RESPOND IN KIND.

YOU'RE COMPLETELY BONKERS, YOU KNOW.

WHAT?!? HOW **DARE** YOU CHEAPEN THE POLITICAL DEBATE WITH YOUR **HATE-FILLED RHETORIC!** YOU DEMOCRATS ARE SO FILLED WITH **RAGE** ALL YOU CAN DO IS **SPEW BILE** BLAH BLAH BLAH... AH BLAH BLAH B... H

SEE? IT ALL MAKES **PERFECT SENSE...**

TOM TOMORROW©2004

THIS MODERN WORLD

by TOM TOMORROW

THIS MODERN WORLD

by TOM TOMORROW

A BRIEF HISTORY OF MARRIAGE IN AMERICA

"After more than two centuries of American jurisprudence...a few judges and local authorities are presuming to change the most fundamental institution of civilization."
--George W. Bush

IN REVOLUTIONARY TIMES, A WIFE EFFECTIVELY BECAME HER HUSBAND'S PROPERTY, WITH FEW RIGHTS OF HER OWN.

MARRIAGE HAS **ALWAYS BEEN** A SACRED BOND BETWEEN A MAN AND HIS **CHATTEL**--AND SO IT WILL **ALWAYS BE!**

IN SLAVEHOLDING STATES, SLAVES-- INCLUDING **FREED** SLAVES--WERE NOT **ALLOWED** TO MARRY.

MARRIAGE HAS **ALWAYS BEEN** A SACRED BOND BETWEEN **TWO WHITE PEOPLE**--AND SO IT WILL **ALWAYS BE!**

AS RECENTLY AS 1967, SIXTEEN STATES REFUSED TO RECOGNIZE MIXED-RACE MARRIAGES.

MARRIAGE HAS **ALWAYS BEEN** A SACRED BOND BETWEEN A MAN AND A WOMAN OF THE **SAME SKIN COLOR**--AND SO IT WILL **ALWAYS BE!**

THE MORE THINGS CHANGE, THE MORE THEY STAY THE SAME.

MARRIAGE HAS **ALWAYS BEEN** A SACRED BOND BETWEEN A HETEROSEXUAL MAN AND A HETEROSEXUAL WOMAN--AND WE'RE GONNA **KEEP** IT THAT WAY! YOU CAN'T GO MESSIN' WITH **TRADITION!**

WHY, PEOPLE MIGHT START MARRYIN' **FARM ANIMALS** AND **HOUSEHOLD APPLIANCES** AND WHO **KNOWS** WHAT! RIGHT, KARL?

ABSOLUTELY, SIR. WE'D BETTER AMEND THE CONSTITUTION--JUST TO BE **SAFE!**

TO DO
1. SCAPEGOAT GAYS

THIS MODERN WORLD

by TOM TOMORROW

MAY, 1972...

LT. BUSH? WE NEED TO HAVE A WORD WITH YOU.

YOU'VE PROBABLY WONDERED WHY YOU WERE BUMPED TO THE FRONT OF THE NATIONAL GUARD WAITING LIST...

UH--NOT REALLY, SIR. YOU KNOW WHO MY **DAD** IS, RIGHT?

THAT HAD **NOTHING** TO DO WITH IT! WE DON'T SHOW FAVORITISM TO THE SONS OF THE ELITE IN **THIS** DEMOCRACY!

THE TRUTH IS, WE HAVE A FAR MORE SERIOUS PROBLEM THAN **VIETNAM**... AND YOUR COUNTRY **NEEDS** YOU!

YOU SEE, SON, WE'RE FIGHTING A SECRET WAR IN OUTER SPACE--AGAINST AN ARMY OF **HIDEOUS SOCIALIST SPACE LIZARDS** BENT ON THE **CONQUEST** OF OUR PLANET!

ONE OF THEIR MAIN WEAPONS IS A **DISORIENTATION RAY**--

--WHICH PRODUCES AN EFFECT NOT UNLIKE **EXTREME DRUNKENNESS**!

WE NEED PILOTS WITH A **HIGH TOLERANCE** FOR THAT SORT OF THING!

AND **THAT'S** WHY WE CHOSE **YOU**!

I'M AT YOUR DISPOSAL, SIRS! BUT--I CAN'T JUST GO **AWOL**!

DON'T WORRY, WE'LL COME UP WITH SOME SORT OF COVER STORY! IT'S NOT LIKE ANYONE'S EVER GOING TO **CARE**!

SOON...

TAKE **THAT**, YA LOUSY **SPACE COMMIES**!

UNITED STATES SPACE DEFENSE

THE HUMAN IS UNAFFECTED BY OUR DISORIENTATION RAY!

THEY MUST HAVE DEVELOPED A DEFENSE! ABORT THE INVASION!

THIRTY-TWO YEARS LATER...

--AND WHERE **WAS** GEORGE BUSH IN 1972?

SIGH...IF ONLY I COULD TELL THEM THE TRUTH, KARL.

THE WORLD MUST NEVER KNOW, SIR.

TOM TOMORROW©2004

THIS MODERN WORLD

by TOM TOMORROW

ANOTHER BEAUTIFUL DAY IN GOTHAM CITY...

--AND THEN, THIS POOR WOMAN STEPPED ON A METAL PLATE ON THE SIDEWALK--AND WAS *ELEC-TROCUTED!*

I SWEAR, YOU NEVER KNOW *WHAT* THIS CITY IS GOING TO THROW AT YOU NEXT!

SPARKY--*LOOK OUT!*

WHAT--?

THUNK!

LATER...

WHAT...WHAT HAPPENED?

UH--YOU HAD AN ACCIDENT. LET'S JUST LEAVE IT AT THAT. HOW DO YOU FEEL?

I FEEL--I FEEL--

--I FEEL *GREAT!* MY *GOD!* SUDDENLY IT'S *ALL SO CLEAR!!*

WHAT, SPARKY? WHAT *IS* IT?

THE PRESIDENT *IS* A UNITER, NOT A DIVIDER! AND YOU *ARE* EITHER WITH HIM OR AGAINST HIM! AND WE *CAN'T* AFFORD TO IGNORE GRAVE AND GATHER-ING THREATS--EVEN WHEN THEY ACTUALLY POSE *NO THREAT WHATSOEVER!*

DON'T YOU *SEE*--?

UM--NOT REALLY--

THE SUM OF *ALL WISDOM* IS CONTAINED--

--IN *REPUBLICAN TALKING POINTS!*

SPARKY, YOU'RE SCARING ME.

OUT OF MY *WAY,* BUSH-HATER! I'VE GOT *WORK* TO DO!

TO BE CONTINUED...

TOM TOMORROW©2004

THIS MODERN WORLD

by TOM TOMORROW

IN A STUNNING TURNAROUND, *SPARKY* BECOMES A DYED-IN-THE-WOOL *REPUBLICAN!*

YOU SEE, SEAN, I *USED* TO BE A LOONY LEFTIST, BUT THEN I REALIZED--YOU'RE EITHER WITH PRESIDENT BUSH--OR YOU SUPPORT THE *WHOLESALE DESTRUCTION* OF *WESTERN CIVILIZATION!* IT'S JUST THAT SIMPLE!

WHAT BROUGHT YOU AROUND, SPARKSTER? WERE YOU *"HANNITIZED"?*

ACTUALLY, SEAN, I WAS HIT ON THE HEAD BY A FALLING TOILET.

OH.

HIS HASTILY-GHOSTWRITTEN MEMOIR (*"LIBERALS ARE TRAITOROUS SCUM FOR WHOM HANGING IS TOO GOOD"*) SHOOTS TO THE TOP OF THE BEST-SELLER LIST--WITH A LITTLE HELP FROM HIS NEW CONSERVATIVE FRIENDS!

ANOTHER BULK SALE, SPARKSTER! RICHARD MELLON SCAIFE JUST BOUGHT FIFTEEN THOUSAND COPIES--TO INSULATE HIS *ATTIC!*

HAH! MATCH *THAT*, AL FRANKEN!

LIBERALS ARE TRAITOROUS SCUM FOR WHOM HANGING IS TOO GOOD

SPARKY T. PENGUIN

HE QUICKLY BECOMES THE TOAST OF THE CONSERVATIVE *ELITE!*

--YOU SEE, POOR PEOPLE ARE BOTH LAZY *AND* STUPID!--AND DON'T GET ME STARTED ON THE *FRENCH!*

HA, HA!

HA, HA!

HIS SCINTILLATING WIT IS RIVALLED ONLY BY HIS KEEN INTELLECT!

YOU KNOW IF HE'S *SINGLE?*

MEANWHILE, THE OBSCURE LEFT-WING CARTOON AT WHICH HE WAS FORMERLY EMPLOYED DESPERATELY TRIES TO GROOM A *REPLACEMENT...*

OKAY, BLINKY--I KNOW YOU'RE A VERY NICE DOG--BUT WE NEED *SOMEONE* TO PROVIDE OUR READERS WITH THE CAUSTIC COMMENTARY THEY'VE COME TO EXPECT! OUR LIVELIHOODS *DEPEND* ON IT!

AHEM! WELL--GEORGE BUSH'S POLICIES AREN'T REALLY *MY* CUP OF TEA--BUT OF COURSE, REASONABLE PEOPLE CAN *ALWAYS* DISAGREE!

SIGH...I WONDER IF "MALLARD FILLMORE" HAS ANY OPENINGS...

TOM TOMORROW©2004

THIS MODERN WORLD

by TOM TOMORROW

SLIME AND DEFEND

A HIGH-RANKING INSIDER RELEASES A HARSHLY CRITICAL MEMOIR.

SIR--WHATEVER INSPIRED YOU TO WRITE A BOOK DENOUNCING YOUR **OWN ADMINISTRATION?**

WELL, LESLIE, WE REALLY **ARE** A BUNCH OF INCOMPETENT BUFFOONS--AND I JUST COULDN'T KEEP QUIET **ANY LONGER!**

WE'RE A BUNCH OF INCOMPETENT BUFFOONS
GEORGE W. BUSH

THE ADMINISTRATION GOES ON THE ATTACK.

THE PRESIDENT IS SIMPLY DISGRUNTLED. AND EVERYONE KNOWS YOU CAN'T TRUST A DISGRUNTLED PERSON!

WHY IS HE DISGRUNTLED, SCOTT?

ER--BECAUSE HE **LACKS GRUNTLEDNESS!**

THE WHITE
WASH

THE AUTHOR'S ALLEGATIONS ARE FLATLY DENIED.

MR. RUMSFELD, IT SAYS HERE THAT YOU ARE A **BIPEDAL, CARBON-BASED LIFE FORM!**

WELL, THAT'S SIMPLY NOT **TRUE!** END OF **DISCUSSION!**

DO PEOPLE WRITE CRAZY THINGS?

THEY SURE **DO!**

HIS MOTIVES ARE IMPUGNED.

MR. BUSH IS CLEARLY TRYING TO DISTANCE HIMSELF FROM AN INCREASINGLY UNPOPULAR ADMINISTRATION! THIS IS NOTHING MORE THAN A **CYNICAL ELECTION-YEAR PLOY!**

AND HE'S JUST IN IT FOR THE MONEY.

THAT TOO.

HIS EXPERTISE IS QUESTIONED.

LOOK, THE GUY'S JUST A **FIGUREHEAD!** HE HAS ABSOLUTELY **NO IDEA** WHAT'S GOING ON AROUND HIM!

HE'S **TOTALLY** OUT OF THE LOOP!

AND OF COURSE, ANY INCONSISTENCIES IN HIS ACCOUNT ARE USED TO DISCREDIT HIM.

HE CLAIMS TO BE "PRESIDENT"-- BUT HE ACTUALLY **LOST** THE POPULAR VOTE!

SO WHY SHOULD ANYONE BELIEVE ANYTHING **ELSE** HE SAYS?

YOU **SAID** IT, RUSH!

TOM TOMORROW©2004

THIS MODERN WORLD

by TOM TOMORROW

Panel 1: IF THERE'S ANOTHER TERROR ATTACK BEFORE THE ELECTION, IT WILL MEAN THAT THE TERRORISTS *WANT* GEORGE BUSH TO *LOSE!*

WE'LL *HAVE* TO VOTE REPUBLICAN--OR ELSE IT WILL BE A VICTORY FOR *TERROR!*

Panel 2: BUT WHAT IF *THAT'S* WHAT THEY *WANT*? WHAT IF THEY'RE ACTUALLY AFRAID *KERRY* WILL WIN--AND BY VOTING FOR BUSH, WE PLAY *RIGHT INTO THEIR HANDS?*

Panel 3: OR--WHAT IF THERE'S *NOT* AN ATTACK BETWEEN NOW AND NOVEMBER? WOULD THAT MEAN THAT THEY *DO* WANT KERRY *NOT TO WIN?*

OR THAT THEY DON'T *NOT* WANT BUSH NOT TO *LOSE?*

Panel 4: *MAYBE* IT WOULD MEAN THAT THEY WANT *US* TO THINK THAT *THEY* THINK THAT *WE* THINK THAT *THEY* THINK THAT AN ATTACK *WOULDN'T* RALLY VOTERS BEHIND BUSH!

BUT--THAT *MIGHT* BE WHAT THEY'RE HOPING WE *WON'T* THINK!

HOW CAN WE *EVER* FIGURE THIS OUT?

Panel 5: I DON'T KNOW--BUT IF WE *DON'T* MAKE OUR ELECTORAL DECISIONS BASED ON WHAT THEY *DON'T WANT US NOT TO DO--*

--THEN THE TERRORISTS *HAVEN'T ALREADY NOT WON!*

Panel 6: OR SOMETHING LIKE THAT.

I'M SO CONFUSED.

MAYBE THEY'RE FOR *NADER!*

TOM TOMORROW©2004

THIS MODERN WORLD

by TOM TOMORROW

TALKING POINTS

WE'RE *HAPPY* TO COOPERATE WITH THE 9/11 COMMISSION--

--BUT WHAT'S DONE IS *DONE!* AMERICANS NEED TO LOOK TO THE *FUTURE,* NOT THE *PAST!*

UNLESS YOU WANT TO BLAME THE *CLINTON ADMINISTRATION* FOR SOMETHING! THEN IT'S *OKAY* TO LOOK TO THE PAST!

RIGHT! AND AS FAR AS LOOKING TO THE *FUTURE* GOES--

--WELL, YOU CERTAINLY DON'T WANT TO GET *CARRIED AWAY!* AFTER ALL, THINGS DON'T ALWAYS TURN OUT THE WAY YOU *EXPECT!*

TAKE FALLUJAH--*PLEASE!*

HEH, HEH! YOU CAN'T SAY I DON'T HAVE A SENSE OF *HUMOR!*

AHEM! SO, TO SUMMARIZE: LOOKING TO THE PAST IS *BAD*--UNLESS YOU'RE LOOKING BACK FOUR YEARS OR *LONGER*--

--AND LOOKING AHEAD IS *GOOD*--UNLESS YOU GET ALL FIXATED ON THINGS GOIN' *WRONG*--

--IN WHICH CASE, IT'S *BAD.*

ACTUALLY, WE'D MOSTLY PREFER IT IF YOU'D JUST STARE DOWN AT YOUR SHOES AND MIND YOUR OWN BUSINESS.

IT'S THE *PA-TRIOTIC* THING TO DO!

YOU *DO* LOVE AMERICA, DON'T YOU?

TOM TOMORROW©2004

THIS MODERN WORLD

by TOM TOMORROW

ACTIONABLE INTELLIGENCE
PART ONE: AUGUST 6, 2001

HERE'S TODAY'S P.D.B., SIR--"BIN LADEN DETERMINED TO STRIKE IN U.S!"

HMMM...PREPARATIONS FOR HIJACKING--EXPLOSIVES--FEDERAL BUILDINGS--NEW YORK--BLAH BLAH BLAH--

GENERIC PRESIDENTIAL ADVISOR #1

GENERIC PRESIDENTIAL ADVISOR #2

--THIS IS ALL PRETTY VAGUE, FELLAS! I NEED DETAILS! I WANT TO KNOW EXACTLY WHAT HE'S GOING TO DO AND EXACTLY WHEN HE'S GOING TO DO IT!

UH--I'M AFRAID OUR INFORMATION'S NOT THAT PRECISE, SIR.

WELL, WITHOUT SPECIFIC, CREDIBLE, WELL-SOURCED INTELLIGENCE, THERE'S ABSOLUTELY NOTHING I CAN DO! ZIP! ZILCH! NADA!

NOW IF YOU BOYS WILL EXCUSE ME, I'M SUPPOSED TO BE ON VACATION HERE!

YES, SIR.

SORRY TO BOTHER YOU, SIR.

PART TWO: EARLY FALL, 2002

WE DON'T REALLY HAVE ANY EVIDENCE, SIR--BUT AHMED CHALABI KNOWS A GUY WHO KNOWS A GUY WHO HAS A FRIEND WHO SAYS SADDAM DEFINITELY HAS WEAPONS OF MASS DESTRUCTION!

GOOD ENOUGH FOR ME! EVIDENCE, SCHMEVIDENCE--WE'RE GOIN' TO WAR!

YES, SIR.

VERY GOOD, SIR.

...AND THE REST IS HISTORY!

TOM TOMORROW©2004

THIS MODERN WORLD

by TOM TOMORROW

AN EMERGENCY MEETING AT "THIS MODERN WORLD" CORPORATE HQ...

NOW THAT SPARKY'S A *REPUBLICAN*, WE NEED A *NEW* MASCOT TO PROVIDE CAUSTIC COMMENTARY-- *A.S.A.P!*

I'LL PUT AN AD ON CRAIG'S LIST.

DON'T BOTHER--I THINK *BLINKY* WILL BE ABLE TO FILL IN...

BLINKY? ARE YOU *NUTS*? BLINKY IS A *VERY NICE DOG* WHO'S NEVER HAD A STRONG OPINION IN HIS *LIFE*! HE DOESN'T HAVE AN ANGRY BONE IN HIS *BODY*!

ER--YES, WELL--

UNBELIEVABLE!!

HAVE YOU PEOPLE *SEEN* THE NEWS LATELY? ACCORDING TO BOB WOODWARD, BUSH TOLD SAUDI *PRINCE BANDAR* WE WERE GOING TO WAR TWO DAYS BEFORE HE TOLD HIS *OWN SECRETARY OF STATE*!

?

NOT ONLY *THAT*--BUT *BANDAR* APPARENTLY SAID THE SAUDIS WOULD LOWER OIL PRICES BEFORE THE ELECTION--TO HELP BUSH *WIN*! IN OTHER WORDS, THE PRESIDENT OF THE UNITED STATES IS *CONSPIRING* WITH A *FOREIGN GOVERNMENT* TO INFLUENCE OUR DEMOCRATIC PROCESS! IT'S AN *OUTRAGE*!

NOW IF YOU'LL *EXCUSE* ME, I'M GONNA GO FIND THAT TURNCOAT *PENGUIN* AND KICK HIS SKINNY BUTT BACK TO *ANTARCTICA*!

SLAM!!

UH-- BOB?

STEROIDS. BEEN SLIPPING THEM INTO HIS DINNER BOWL FOR A COUPLE OF WEEKS NOW.

I'LL GO PLACE THAT AD.

GOOD IDEA.

TOM TOMORROW©2004

THIS MODERN WORLD

by TOM TOMORROW

Panel 1:

IT WAS THE ANNIVERSARY OF THE MOST POORLY CONCEIVED PHOTO OP SINCE MICHAEL DUKAKIS CLIMBED INTO A TANK.

NO DOUBT ABOUT IT--THIS IS GONNA MAKE A *GREAT* CAMPAIGN COMMERCIAL!

WHAT COULD GO *WRONG*?

MISSION ACCOMPLISHED

Panel 2:

IT WAS THE WEEK THAT THE PRESIDENT AND VICE-PRESIDENT APPEARED TOGETHER BEFORE THE 9/11 COMMISSION.

AND PLEASE--NO MORE *VENTRILOQUISM* JOKES!

AND PLEASE--NO MORE VENTRILOQUISM JOKES!

Panel 3:

AND IT WAS THE WEEK THE SUPREME COURT HEARD THE CASE OF CHENEY'S SECRET ENERGY TASK FORCE.

WE'LL GO *HUNTING* FOR THE TRUTH--AND I ASSURE YOU, WE WILL NOT *DUCK* THE ISSUES!

QUACK, QUACK!

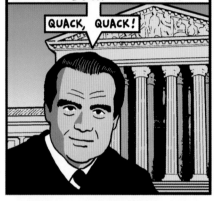

Panel 4:

CLEARLY A DISTRACTION WAS URGENTLY REQUIRED.

I THINK WE SHOULD GO AFTER KERRY'S *WAR RECORD*! AFTER ALL--*I'M* THE "*WAR PRESIDENT*"!

ER--YES SIR. EXCELLENT IDEA, SIR.

Panel 5:

AND COINCIDENTALLY ENOUGH, ONE SOON TURNED UP...AS THE MEDIA SUDDENLY BECAME FIXATED ON *RIBBONGATE*...

DID JOHN KERRY THROW AWAY HIS *RIBBONS*--OR HIS *MEDALS*? AND WERE THEY REALLY *HIS*--OR JUST *CLEVER FORGERIES*?

AND DOES THIS *PROVE* THAT JOHN KERRY HATES AMERICA--OR IS THERE STILL A *SHADOW* OF A DOUBT?

Action McNews

Panel 6:

MEANWHILE, CONSERVATIVES PROVED ONCE AGAIN THAT THEY ARE CHEERFULLY UNBURDENED BY CONSISTENCY.

WHO *CARES* WHAT THE PRESIDENT KNEW--OR WHEN HE KNEW IT?

WE'RE AT *WAR*! WE CAN'T WASTE TIME REHASHING THE *PAST*!

UNLESS YOU'RE TALKING ABOUT JOHN KERRY'S PAST.

RIGHT. THEN WE'LL MAKE TIME.

NEXT WEEK: A BRAND NEW WEEK!

TOM TOMORROW©2004

THIS MODERN WORLD

by TOM TOMORROW

IT'S BEEN A YEAR SINCE THE "MISSION ACCOMPLISHED" SPEECH.

CASUALTIES CONTINUE TO MOUNT.

IMAGES OF AMERICANS TORTURING IRAQI PRISONERS HAVE FURTHER INFLAMED ANTI-AMERICAN SENTIMENT.

A MAJORITY OF IRAQIS NOW VIEW US AS "OCCU-PIERS" RATHER THAN "LIBERATORS."

WE'RE SUPPOSED TO HAND OVER CONTROL IN LESS THAN TWO MONTHS.

NOBODY SEEMS TO KNOW WHO WE'RE HANDING IT *TO*.

THE ADMINISTRATION NEVER HAD A REALISTIC POSTWAR PLAN--AND NOW WE'RE PAYING THE PRICE.

WITH THINGS GOING *THIS* BADLY, I GUESS IT'S CLEAR WHAT WE NEED TO DO ON ELECTION DAY.

VOTE FOR *GEORGE W. BUSH*, OF COURSE!

DAMN *STRAIGHT!* WE *CAN'T* SWITCH HORSES IN *MIDSTREAM!*

FOUR MORE YEARS, BABY!

THERE'S NO *TELL-ING* WHAT KIND OF MESS *JOHN KERRY* MIGHT GET US INTO!

I SHUD-DER TO *THINK* OF IT.

TOM TOMORROW©2004

85

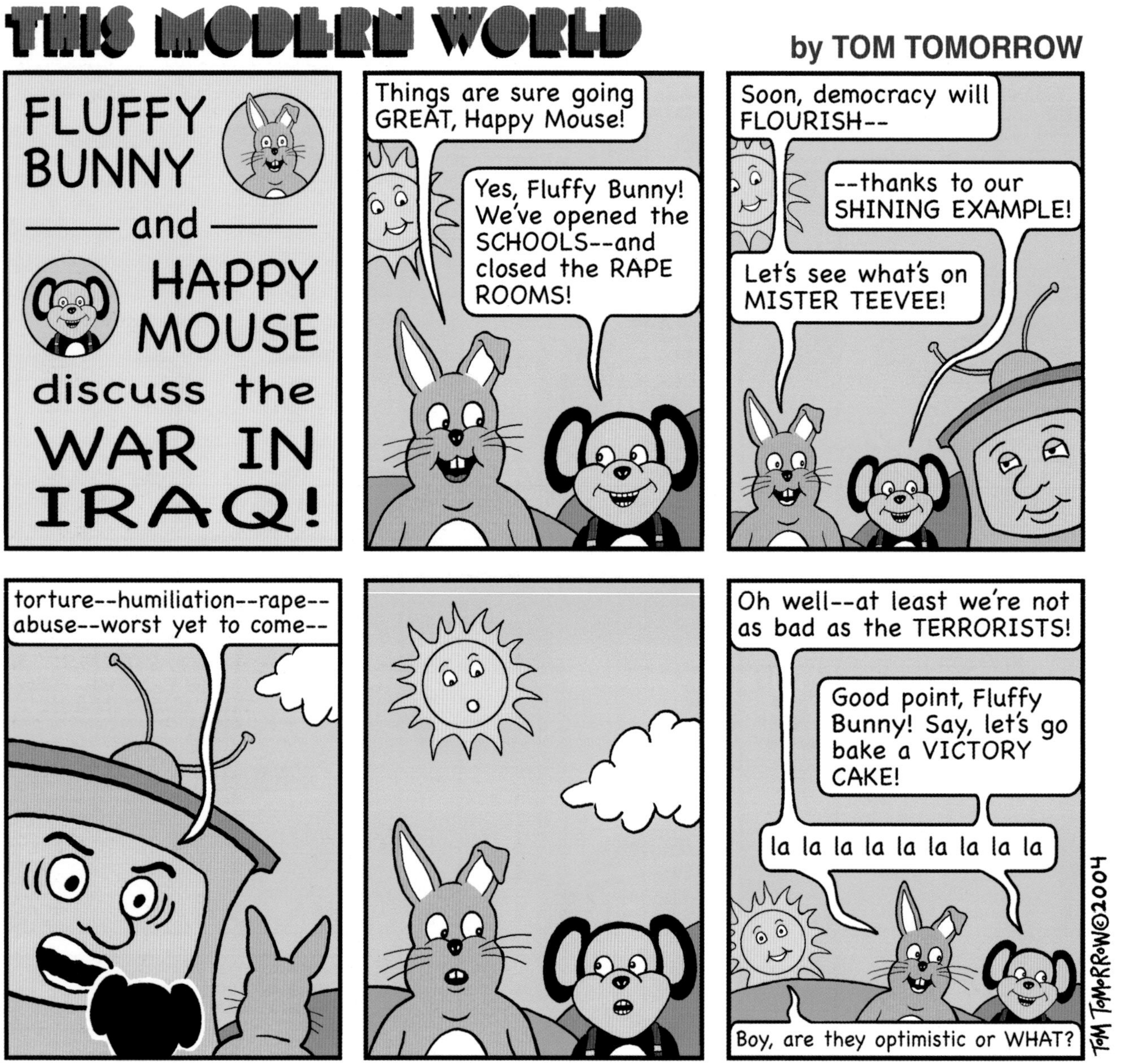
THIS MODERN WORLD
by TOM TOMORROW
FLUFFY BUNNY and HAPPY MOUSE discuss the WAR IN IRAQ!
Things are sure going GREAT, Happy Mouse!
Yes, Fluffy Bunny! We've opened the SCHOOLS--and closed the RAPE ROOMS!
Soon, democracy will FLOURISH--
--thanks to our SHINING EXAMPLE!
Let's see what's on MISTER TEEVEE!
torture--humiliation--rape--abuse--worst yet to come--
Oh well--at least we're not as bad as the TERRORISTS!
Good point, Fluffy Bunny! Say, let's go bake a VICTORY CAKE!
la la la la la la la la la
Boy, are they optimistic or WHAT?
TOM TOMORROW©2004

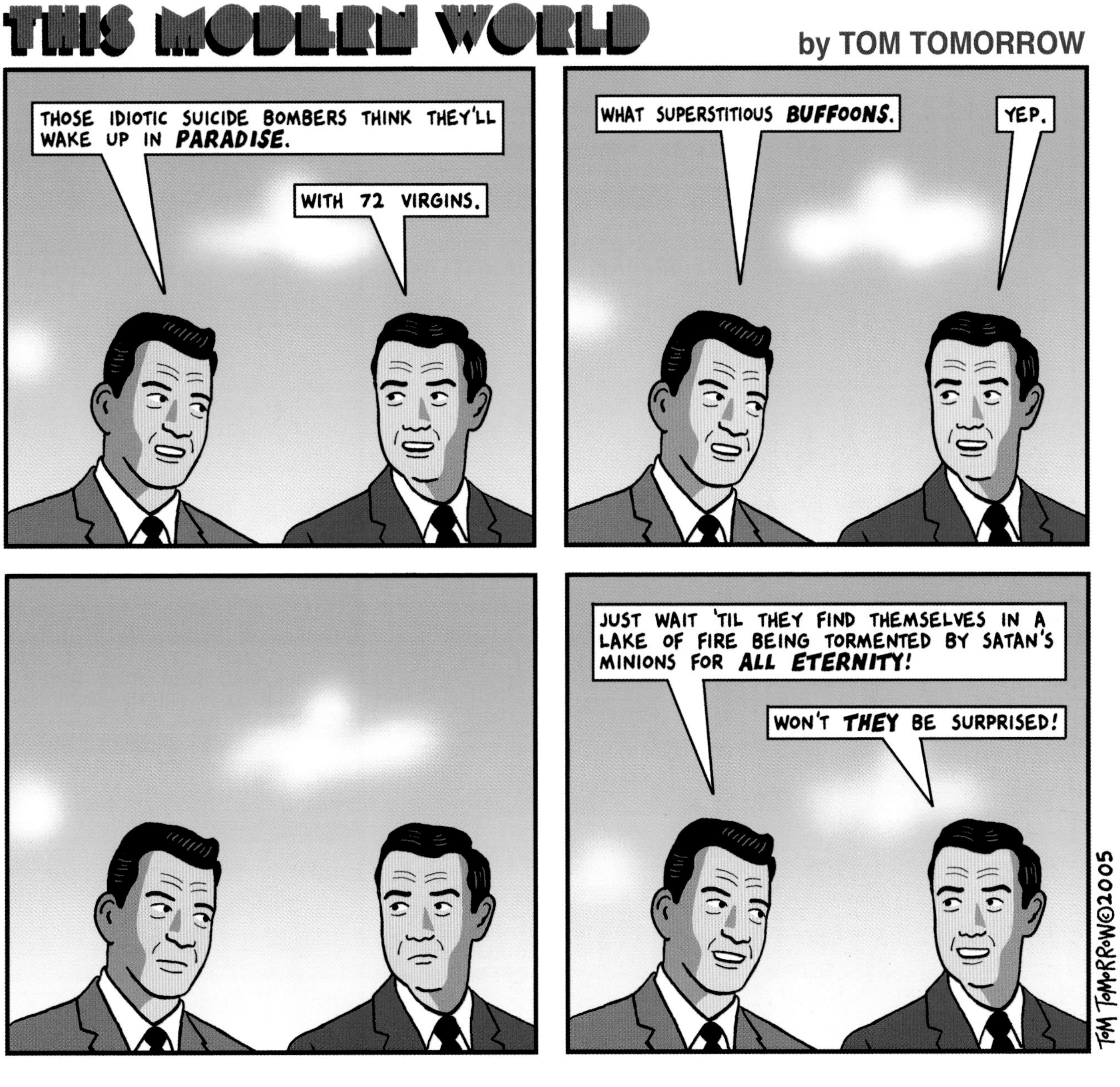
THIS MODERN WORLD
by TOM TOMORROW
THOSE IDIOTIC SUICIDE BOMBERS THINK THEY'LL WAKE UP IN PARADISE.
WITH 72 VIRGINS.
WHAT SUPERSTITIOUS BUFFOONS.
YEP.
JUST WAIT 'TIL THEY FIND THEMSELVES IN A LAKE OF FIRE BEING TORMENTED BY SATAN'S MINIONS FOR ALL ETERNITY!
WON'T THEY BE SURPRISED!
TOM TOMORROW©2005

THIS MODERN WORLD

by TOM TOMORROW

DEFINING DEVIANCY DOWN

SENATOR INHOFE INTRODUCED THE RATIONALE.

AMERICAN TROOPS MAY HAVE RAPED, TORTURED, BEATEN AND HUMILIATED IRAQI PRISONERS--

--BUT WE'RE **NOT AS BAD AS SADDAM!**

YOU'VE GOT TO KEEP THINGS IN **PERSPECTIVE!**

OTHERS QUICKLY LATCHED ONTO IT.

MY CLIENT MAY OR MAY NOT BE A LOATHSOME CHILD MOLESTER--

--BUT THE **IMPORTANT** THING TO REMEMBER IS THAT HE'S **NOT SADDAM HUSSEIN!**

GOOD POINT!

I HADN'T THOUGHT OF IT LIKE **THAT!**

BEFORE LONG, IT WAS EVERYWHERE.

BOSS, IT'S TRUE THAT I EMBEZZLED A HALF MILLION DOLLARS--BUT AS A PATRIOTIC, RED-BLOODED AMERICAN, I'M **SURE** YOU'LL UNDERSTAND THAT I'M **NOT AS BAD AS SADDAM!**

WELL, SINCE YOU PUT IT THAT WAY, LET'S JUST FORGET THE WHOLE THING!

BUT WIDESPREAD USE BEGAN TO DIMINISH ITS EFFECTIVNESS.

I'M NOT AS BAD AS SADDAM!

WELL, NEITHER AM **I!**

I'M **MORE** NOT AS BAD AS SADDAM THAN **YOU** ARE!

TELL IT TO THE HAND, GIRLFRIEND!

FORTUNATELY, AMERICANS SOON REALIZED THERE WERE **PLENTY** OF PEOPLE TO BE NOT AS BAD AS.

HONEY, I CAN'T DENY THAT I HAD A THREESOME WITH YOUR SISTER AND YOUR BEST FRIEND--BUT THE **IMPORTANT** THING TO REMEMBER--

--IS THAT I'M NOT AS BAD AS **OSAMA BIN LADEN!** OR **JOSEF STALIN!** OR **JEFFREY DAHMER!**

YOU'VE GOT TO KEEP THINGS IN **PERSPECTIVE!**

TOM TOMORROW©2004

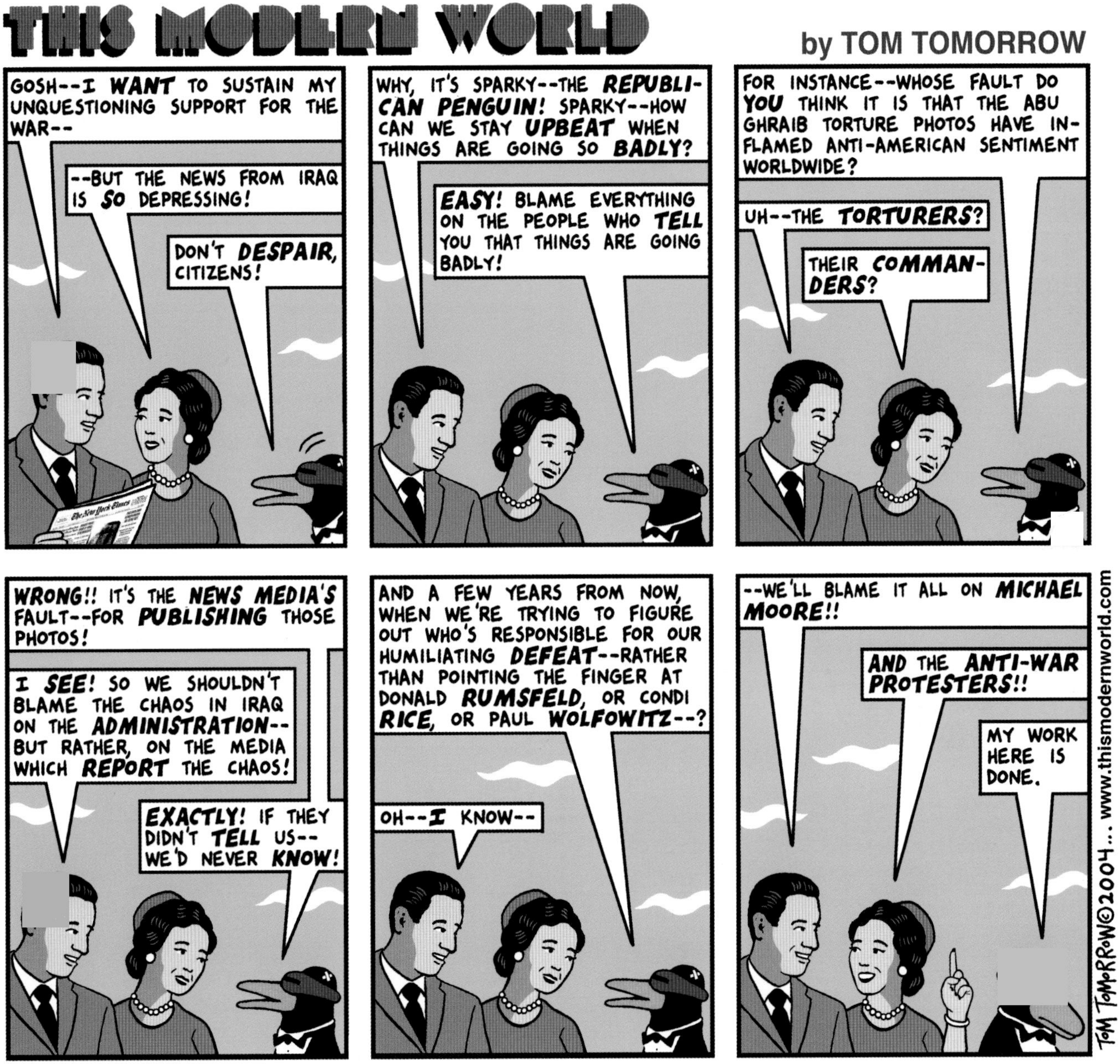
THIS MODERN WORLD
by TOM TOMORROW
GOSH--I WANT TO SUSTAIN MY UNQUESTIONING SUPPORT FOR THE WAR--
--BUT THE NEWS FROM IRAQ IS SO DEPRESSING!
DON'T DESPAIR, CITIZENS!
WHY, IT'S SPARKY--THE REPUBLICAN PENGUIN! SPARKY--HOW CAN WE STAY UPBEAT WHEN THINGS ARE GOING SO BADLY?
EASY! BLAME EVERYTHING ON THE PEOPLE WHO TELL YOU THAT THINGS ARE GOING BADLY!
FOR INSTANCE--WHOSE FAULT DO YOU THINK IT IS THAT THE ABU GHRAIB TORTURE PHOTOS HAVE INFLAMED ANTI-AMERICAN SENTIMENT WORLDWIDE?
UH--THE TORTURERS?
THEIR COMMANDERS?
WRONG!! IT'S THE NEWS MEDIA'S FAULT--FOR PUBLISHING THOSE PHOTOS!
I SEE! SO WE SHOULDN'T BLAME THE CHAOS IN IRAQ ON THE ADMINISTRATION--BUT RATHER, ON THE MEDIA WHICH REPORT THE CHAOS!
EXACTLY! IF THEY DIDN'T TELL US--WE'D NEVER KNOW!
AND A FEW YEARS FROM NOW, WHEN WE'RE TRYING TO FIGURE OUT WHO'S RESPONSIBLE FOR OUR HUMILIATING DEFEAT--RATHER THAN POINTING THE FINGER AT DONALD RUMSFELD, OR CONDI RICE, OR PAUL WOLFOWITZ--?
OH--I KNOW--
--WE'LL BLAME IT ALL ON MICHAEL MOORE!!
AND THE ANTI-WAR PROTESTERS!!
MY WORK HERE IS DONE.
TOM TOMORROW©2004... www.thismodernworld.com

THIS MODERN WORLD

by TOM TOMORROW

CONSERVATIVES REMAIN **VERY SUSPICIOUS** OF THE NEW YORK TIMES' PRE-WAR COVERAGE OF IRAQ...

I THINK THEY DELIBERATELY **UNDERSTATED** THE THREAT POSED BY SADDAM--TO MAKE THE PRESIDENT LOOK **FOOLISH** FOR TAKING US TO **WAR!**

WHAT **ELSE** COULD EXPLAIN SUCH ONE-SIDED REPORTING?

DAMN THE DEVIOUS LIBERAL MEDIA!

IN REALITY, OF COURSE, THE NEW YORK TIMES HELPED TO **BOLSTER** THE CASE FOR WAR...RUNNING NUMEROUS FRONT-PAGE STORIES ABOUT IRAQI WMD'S BY REPORTER JUDITH MILLER--WHOSE PRIMARY SOURCE WAS THE BUSH ADMINISTRATION'S THEN-FAVORITE IRAQI EXILE, **AHMED CHALABI**...

JUDY--YOU **MUST** BELIEVE ME! SADDAM'S GENETICISTS HAVE CREATED A SECRET ARMY OF **GIANT MUTATED LIZARDS** THAT, UM, SHOOT **LASER BEAMS!** OUT OF THEIR **EYEBALLS!**

SOUNDS LIKE AN ABOVE-THE-FOLD **SCOOP** TO **ME!**

AND ONLY AFTER CHALABI'S RECENT FALL FROM GRACE DID THE TIMES **REVISIT** THOSE STORIES...CONCEDING THAT THEY MAY HAVE CONTAINED A FEW **SLIGHT** INACCURACIES...

AHEM--YES--FOR INSTANCE, NO LASER-EYED MUTANT LIZARDS HAVE **ACTUALLY** BEEN DISCOVERED IN IRAQ.

NOR DOES IT APPEAR THAT SADDAM **REALLY** HAD A TIME MACHINE WITH WHICH HE COULD TRAVEL INTO THE PAST AND PREVENT THE PRESIDENT'S PARENTS FROM EVER **MEETING**.

THE NEW YORK TIMES REGRETS THE ERRORS.

NONETHELESS...CONSERVATIVES REMAIN **VERY SUSPICIOUS** OF THE NEW YORK TIMES' PRE-WAR COVERAGE OF IRAQ...

I THINK THEY DELIBERATELY **OVERSTATED** THE THREAT POSED BY SADDAM--TO MAKE THE PRESIDENT LOOK **FOOLISH** WHEN NO GIANT MUTATED LIZARDS WERE **FOUND!**

WHAT **ELSE** COULD EXPLAIN SUCH ONE-SIDED REPORTING?

DAMN THE DEVIOUS LIBERAL MEDIA!

TOM TOMORROW©2004

THIS MODERN WORLD

by TOM TOMORROW

Panel 1: WELCOME BACK TO OUR ONGOING *RONALD REAGAN COVERAGE!* IF YOU'RE JUST JOINING US, WE'VE BEEN DISCUSSING PRESIDENT REAGAN'S *BOUNDLESS OPTIMISM!*

BOY, HAVE WE *EVER!* FOR ABOUT A *WEEK,* NOW!

Panel 2: WELL, HE HAD A LOT OF OPTIMISM TO *DISCUSS!*

HE SURE *DID!* THROUGH *DEFICITS, SCANDALS,* AND *ILLEGAL WARS*--WHEN LIFE HANDED HIM *LEMONS*--

--HE ELIMINATED GOVERNMENT REGULATION OF *LEMONADE FACTORIES!*

Panel 3: TAKE THE *AIDS EPIDEMIC!* WITH TENS OF THOUSANDS DYING FROM A MYSTERIOUS *PLAGUE,* A LESSER MAN MIGHT HAVE SUCCUMBED TO *WORRY*--OR AT LEAST *MILD CONCERN!*

BUT NOT *RONALD REAGAN!* WHY, HE DIDN'T EVEN MENTION AIDS IN *PUBLIC* UNTIL *1987!*

Panel 4: AND IT DIDN'T MATTER *HOW* MANY MEMBERS OF HIS ADMINISTRATION WERE FACING CRIMINAL INDICTMENT-- OR *HOW* MANY MILLIONS WERE WASTED ON THE FANTASY OF A SPACE-BASED MISSILE DEFENSE SYSTEM--

--HE ALWAYS LET A *SMILE* BE *HIS* SPACE UMBRELLA!

Panel 5: YES, FROM ARMS SALES TO *IRAN* TO DEATH SQUADS IN *CENTRAL AMERICA*--FOR HIM, THE KETCHUP BOTTLE WAS ALWAYS *HALF FULL*--

--AND THE *KETCHUP* WAS A *VEGETABLE!*

Panel 6: COMING UP NEXT--A SINGLE WORD THAT *DEFINES* THE REAGAN LEGACY-- AT LEAST AS FAR AS *WE'RE* CONCERNED!

WE'LL GIVE YOU A *HINT*--IT STARTS WITH "OP"--AND ENDS WITH "TIMISM"!

FIRST THESE MESSAGES.

TOM TOMORROW©2004

91

THIS MODERN WORLD

by TOM TOMORROW

LEARNING CURVE

FIRST WE LEARN ABOUT THE ABUSES AT ABU GHRAIB.

HARRUMPH! CLEARLY THE WORK OF A *FEW BAD APPLES!*

CERTAINLY NO WORSE THAN THE *AVERAGE FRATERNITY PRANK!*

THEN WE LEARN THAN DONALD RUMSFELD REQUESTED A REPORT ON THE *LEGALITY OF TORTURE* IN MARCH, 2003.

WELL, THAT DOESN'T *PROVE* ANYTHING!

MAYBE HE WAS SIMPLY DISCUSSING THE MOST RECENT SEASON OF "24" ON AN INTERNET CHAT BOARD SOMEWHERE!

THEN WE LEARN OF JUSTICE DEPARTMENT MEMOS FROM 2002 WHICH DISCUSS THE DEGREE OF SUFFERING *ALLOWABLE* DURING INTERROGATION.

BUT REST ASSURED, THERE IS *NO TRUTH* TO THE RUMOR THAT DETAINEES HAVE BEEN FORCED TO LISTEN TO ME SINGING "LET THE EAGLE SOAR" UNTIL THEY BEG TO HAVE ELECTRODES ATTACHED TO THEIR GENITALS INSTEAD.

BECAUSE THAT WOULD BE WRONG.

THEN WE LEARN THAT IN JANUARY, 2002, RUMSFELD APPROVED THE USE OF DOGS TO INTIMIDATE PRISONERS AT GUANTANAMO--A TACTIC LATER USED AT ABU GHRAIB.

ER--WOULD YOU BELIEVE I WAS REFERRING TO *TRIUMPH, THE INSULT COMIC DOG?*

HIS CLEVER BARBS CAN BE *VERY* INTIMIDATING, YOU KNOW!

WE LEARN MORE AND MORE, ALL OF IT CLEARLY INDICATING THAT THE TORTURE OF DETAINEES WAS AN OFFICIALLY SANCTIONED POLICY.

LOOK, EVERYONE STAYED *WITHIN THE LAW!*

OF COURSE, THE WAY RUMSFELD AND ASHCROFT FIGURE IT, THE LAW IS PRETTY MUCH WHAT WE *SAY* IT IS!

HEH, HEH! MAYBE I SHOULD DECLARE JOHN KERRY AN *ENEMY COMBATANT!*

OOPS! DID I SAY THAT OUT LOUD?

AND SOMEDAY, SOME AMERICAN P.O.W. SOMEWHERE WILL LEARN WHY THE ADMINISTRATION REALLY SHOULD HAVE TRIED TO SET A BETTER EXAMPLE.

TODAY WE WILL STRAP YOU TO A BOARD AND HOLD YOU UNDER WATER UNTIL YOU THINK YOU WILL DIE!*

DO NOT WORRY! YOUR OWN GOVERNMENT SAYS IT IS NOT TORTURE!

THINK OF IT AS A HARMLESS *FRATERNITY PRANK!*

ULP.

*ACTUAL INTERROGATION TECHNIQUE USED AT GUANTANAMO.

TOM TOMORROW©2004

THIS MODERN WORLD

by TOM TOMORROW

IT'S INCREASINGLY CLEAR THAT THE WAR IN IRAQ HAS IN NO WAY DIMINISHED THE THREAT OF TERROR--

WHY DO YOU LIBERALS HATE AMERICA SO MUCH?

OH *NO* YOU DON'T! YOUR SIDE HAS BEEN PULLING OUT THAT SAME EMOTIONALLY-CHARGED NON SEQUITUR FOR THE PAST *THREE YEARS*--AND IT'S *OVER!* YOU'VE RUN IT INTO THE *GROUND!* IT'S NOT GOING TO WORK *ANY MORE!*

NOW AS I WAS *SAYING*--BUSH ACTUALLY *DIVERTED* RESOURCES FROM THE WAR ON TERROR TO PURSUE HIS SINGLE-MINDED OB- SESSION WITH IRAQ--

WHY DO YOU LIBERALS HATE YOUR *MOTHERS* SO MUCH?

WHA-- *WHAT*?

WHY DO YOU HATE YOUR MOTHER? DON'T YOU UNDERSTAND ALL THE *SACRIFICES* SHE MADE FOR YOU?

BUT--BUT--YOU'RE *WRONG!* I *DON'T* HATE MY MOTHER! AND I'LL *PROVE* IT TO YOU! WHY-- I'M GOING TO GO BUY HER AN EXPENSIVE PRESENT--*RIGHT NOW!* AND I'LL SEND *FLOWERS!* AND--AND--

OH. YOU'RE DOING IT AGAIN, AREN'T YOU?

I HAVE NO IDEA WHAT YOU MIGHT BE TALKING ABOUT.

SO--WHY DOES YOUR *MOTHER* HATE AMERICA?

WHAT? SHE *DOESN'T!* SHE-- OH.

TOM TOMORROW ©2004

THIS MODERN WORLD

by TOM TOMORROW

94

THIS MODERN WORLD

by TOM TOMORROW

Panel 1: SO YOU'RE A REPUBLICAN NOW? — YEP.

Panel 2: AND YOU BELIEVE THE WAR IN IRAQ WAS *JUSTIFIED*? — ABSOLUTELY.

Panel 3: WE *HAVE* TO BE PRE-EMPTIVE! LIKE THE PRESIDENT SAYS, WE LEARNED ON 9-11 THAT *OCEANS NO LONGER PROTECT US!*

Panel 4: ER--RIGHT. I REMEMBER HOW SAFE WE ALL FELT BACK DURING THE COLD WAR, WITH THOSE GREAT BIG *OCEANS* KEEPING US SAFE FROM THE THREAT OF NUCLEAR ANNHILATION.

Panel 5:

Panel 6: WHY *DO* YOU HATE AMERICA? — WOW! YOU REALLY *ARE* A REPUBLICAN!

TOM TOMORROW ©2004

THIS MODERN WORLD

by TOM TOMORROW

HE'S NOT JUST A *LIBERAL*--HE'S A

SENSIBLE LIBERAL!

MODERATION IN PURSUIT OF FURTHER MODERATION IS *NO VICE!*

IN THE RUNUP TO WAR, HE CAREFULLY CONSIDERED *ALL SIDES* OF THE *ISSUE.*

GIVEN THE *UNDENIABLE THREAT* POSED BY SADDAM, I FEEL I *MUST* SUPPORT THE WAR!

IT'S THE *SENSIBLE* THING TO DO!

EVEN NOW, HE VIEWS THE ANTI-WAR PROTESTERS WITH *DISDAIN.*

OKAY, SURE, THEY WERE RIGHT AND I WAS WRONG--

--BUT THEY WEREN'T AS *SENSIBLE* AS ME!

OUTSPOKEN CRITICS OF THE ADMINISTRATION MAKE HIM *VERY UNCOMFORTABLE.*

IS IT *REALLY* NECESSARY TO CALL THE PRESIDENT A "LIAR"?

I SHOULD THINK IT WOULD SUFFICE TO GENTLY SUGGEST THAT HE *MAY* BE SOMEWHAT *MISGUIDED!*

HE'S *PARTICULARLY* QUICK TO DISTANCE HIMSELF FROM *MICHAEL MOORE.*

I THINK HIS TACTICS ARE *BAD FOR DEMOCRACY!*

DOESN'T HE *UNDERSTAND?* THE *BEST* WAY TO REACH AMERICANS IS THROUGH *PONDEROUS ESSAYS* IN *OBSCURE POLITICAL JOURNALS!*

YES, HE'S A *SENSIBLE* LIBERAL--

HAVE YOU *HEARD?* BUSH WANTS TO SUSPEND THE *CONSTITUTION* AND DECLARE HIMSELF *DICTATOR-FOR-LIFE!*

WELL THEN--WE NEED TO CONSIDER HIS PROPOSAL ON ITS *MERITS*-- SO WE CAN REACH A *SENSIBLE* CONCLUSION!

--AND HE HAS THE GRATITUDE OF *REPUBLICANS EVERYWHERE.*

TOM TOMORROW©2004

THIS MODERN WORLD

by TOM TOMORROW

OUR STORY SO FAR

THE PRESIDENT WARNS OF AN **IMPENDING THREAT.**

WE HAVE **PROOF** THAT SADDAM IS CREATING AN ARMY OF **GIANT MUTANT LIZARDS** THAT SHOOT **LASER BEAMS** OUT OF THEIR **EYEBALLS!**

WE CAN'T WAIT FOR THE SMOKING GUN TO COME IN THE FORM OF A BUNCH OF **GIANT LIZARDS!**

MEMBERS OF HIS ADMINISTRATION PUT THEIR OWN CREDIBILITY ON THE LINE.

NOT ONLY DOES HE HAVE THE **LIZARDS**--HE ALSO HAS THE CAPABILITY AND INTENT TO MANUFACTURE **UNSTOPPABLE KILLER ROBOTS!**

HONEST!

Unstop... Killer Robot Factories

2002

Decontamination Vehicle   Security

THE PUBLIC GROWS INCREASINGLY FRANTIC.

DO YOU HAVE ANY **IDEA** HOW MUCH DAMAGE AN ARMY OF MUTANT LIZARDS CAN **DO** WITH THEIR LASER-SHOOTING EYEBALLS?

ESPECIALLY IF THEY'RE BACKED UP BY UNSTOPPABLE KILLER ROBOTS!

THE INEVITABLE WAR ENSUES. VICTORY IS QUICKLY DECLARED.

WE HAVE **LIBERATED** THE GRATEFUL, ROSE-PETAL-TOSSING POPULACE OF IRAQ FROM THEIR LIZARD-CREATING OVERLORD!

WE EXPECT TO FIND THE LIZARDS ANY DAY NOW.

A YEAR LATER, PEOPLE ARE STILL DYING.

EVENTUALLY, IT BECOMES POLITICALLY PALATABLE FOR DEMOCRATS TO ACKNOWLEDGE THE OBVIOUS.

WHY--THERE WAS **NEVER** ANY REAL EVIDENCE OF GIANT LIZARDS-- **OR** KILLER ROBOTS!

HAD WE BUT KNOWN THE **TRUTH**, WE SURELY WOULD NOT HAVE VOTED FOR THIS NOW-UNPOPULAR WAR!

REPUBLICANS, MEANWHILE, CONTINUE TO CLUTCH AT STRAWS.

IT SAYS HERE THAT THERE ARE **MANY** SPECIES OF LIZARDS IN IRAQ-- AND SOME OF THEM GROW FAIRLY **LARGE!**

BIG LIZARDS, EH? WELL THEN--THE ENTIRE WAR WAS **TOTALLY JUSTIFIED!** WE WERE **RIGHT** AND THE LEFTIES WERE **WRONG!** THEY SHOULD GET ON THEIR KNEES AND **APOLOGIZE PROFUSELY!** BLAH BLAH BLAH BLAH BLAH BLAH BLAH BLAH BLAH

REPTILES OF THE MIDDLE EAST

THIS MODERN WORLD

by TOM TOMORROW

NOTE: BLINKY THE VERY NICE DOG HAS RECOVERED FROM HIS RECENT STEROID OVERDOSE, AND IS BACK TO NORMAL--JUST IN TIME FOR...

THE VERY NICE DEMOCRATIC CONVENTION

IN KEEPING WITH THE DEMOCRATIC PARTY'S NEWFOUND SENSE OF **UNITY**, THIS MODERN WORLD SENDS THE EVER-OPTIMISTIC **BLINKY** TO **BLOG THE CONVENTION!**

"BLOGGER'S ALLEY," FAR, FAR UP IN THE RAFTERS...

WE HAVE A **VERY NICE VIEW** FROM UP HERE!

I JUST HAVE TO BE CAREFUL NOT TO BUMP MY HEAD ON THE **CEILING!**

BLOGGERS ARE A **BIG STORY** THIS YEAR--POSSIBLY BECAUSE THERE **IS** NO OTHER NEWS...

SO--YOU POST YOUR THOUGHTS AND OPINIONS ON THE **INTERNET**? THAT'S **SO** FASCINATING!

I'M BLOGGING YOU RIGHT NOW!

I'M BLOGGING HIM BLOGGING YOU!

TAP TAP

TAP

TAP

I WISH I HAD THUMBS, SO I COULD BLOG **FASTER!**

NOT THAT THE DEMOCRATS ARE LACKING A **MESSAGE**, OF COURSE! IT'S **SUBTLE**--BUT IF YOU **REALLY PAY ATTENTION**, YOU MIGHT NOTICE IT!

WAR HERO   WAR H

HEY DID WE MENTION HE'S A WAR HERO

WAR HERO   WAR

VAR HERO   HERO

HERO

AND LET'S NOT FORGET THE RESCUE OF **LICORICE THE HAMSTER!**

BUT IT'S REALLY ONE OF JOHN KERRY'S **OTHER** ATTRIBUTES WHICH BRINGS THE VARIOUS WINGS OF THE PARTY TOGETHER THIS YEAR LIKE **NEVER BEFORE**--

--HE IS **NOT** GEORGE BUSH!

AND HE'S **VERY GOOD** AT IT!

OF COURSE, AT ANY CONVENTION, A FEW SNAFUS ARE INEVITABLE...LIKE TRYING TO CRAM SO MANY PEOPLE INTO THE CONVENTION CENTER THAT THE FIRE DEPARTMENT DECIDES TO LOCK DOWN THE BUILDING, TRAPPING A THOUSAND OR SO PEOPLE OUTSIDE DURING JOHN KERRY'S ACCEPTANCE SPEECH...

OH WELL! I'M SURE IT WAS A VERY NICE SPEECH!

WEST EN RANCE

CAN I GO TO A V.I.P. PARTY NOW?

NO.

THIS MODERN WORLD

Panel 1:
REPUBLICANS SAY JOHN KERRY IS *OUT OF TOUCH* BECAUSE HE IS *RICH*.

A SON OF WEALTH AND PRIVILEGE LIKE JOHN KERRY CAN *NEVER* UNDERSTAND ORDINARY AMERICANS LIKE *WE* DO!

WE SPEAK THEIR *LANGUAGE*! WE ARE *JUST LIKE THEM*!

EXCEPT WITH MORE MONEY.

Panel 2:
THEY SAY JOHN KERRY SHOULD PRIMARILY BE VIEWED WITH *DERISION*.

HA, HA! DID YOU *SEE* HIM IN THAT NASA SUIT?

THE VOTERS AREN'T GOING TO TRUST A CANDIDATE WHO MAKES AN ASS OF HIMSELF PLAYING *DRESS UP*!

SOMEONE SHOULD TELL HIM HALLOWEEN IS--UM--*SEVERAL MONTHS* AWAY!

Panel 3:
SOME REPUBLICANS EVEN SUGGEST THAT THE *DEMOCRATS* ARE PLANNING TO *STEAL THE ELECTION* IN *FLORIDA*.

THEY CAN'T BE *TRUSTED*! ALL THEY CARE ABOUT IS *WINNING*!

THEY'RE CAPABLE OF *ANYTHING*!

THEY'D PROBABLY TAKE IT ALL THE WAY TO THE *SUPREME COURT* IF THEY HAD TO!

Panel 4:
IN SHORT...REPUBLICANS SEEM TO BE A LITTLE *CONFUSED* LATELY...

IF *WE'RE* ELECTED, *WE* WON'T TAKE THE COUNTRY TO WAR UNDER FALSE PREMISES!

AND *OUR* CANDIDATE WON'T BE STRUTTING AROUND LIKE AN IDIOT IN ANY DAMN *FLIGHT SUIT*! HA, HA, HA!

HA, HA--

HEY, WAIT A MINUTE.

TOM TOMORROW©2004

99

THIS MODERN WORLD

by TOM TOMORROW

Panel 1:
GOOD NEWS--SPARKY SEEMS TO HAVE RECOVERED FROM HIS HEAD INJURY!

THEY SAY THEY FOUND YOU WANDERING AROUND A WAL-MART IN PEORIA, ILLINOIS--MUTTERING TO YOURSELF ABOUT THE *OLSEN TWINS!*

THEY *ARE* VERY *NICE* TWINS!

Panel 2:
I HAVE NO IDEA HOW I ENDED UP *THERE*...THE LAST THING *I* REMEMBER IS WALKING DOWN THE STREET WITH BLINKY AND GETTING HIT ON THE HEAD WITH SOMETHING...THE LAST FIVE MONTHS ARE A *TOTAL BLANK*...

AHEM.

YES. WELL.

Panel 3:
SO WHAT DID *I* MISS? HAS RUMSFELD *RESIGNED*? IS CHENEY UNDER *INVESTIGATION*? HAS BUSH'S FAILURE TO REPORT FOR NATIONAL GUARD DUTY IN ALABAMA BECOME A *MAJOR CAMPAIGN ISSUE*?

ER--

Panel 4:
--ACTUALLY, PEOPLE ARE PAYING MORE ATTENTION TO A GROUP OF WELL-FUNDED POLITICAL OPERATIVES WHO SERVED IN VIETNAM AT THE SAME TIME AS *JOHN KERRY!*

THEY SAY *HIS* WAR RECORD HAS BEEN *SOMEWHAT EXAGGERATED!*

Panel 5:
UH--LET ME GET THIS STRAIGHT. BUSH AVOIDED VIETNAM ENTIRELY BY PULLING STRINGS TO GET INTO THE NATIONAL GUARD--AND *THEN* WENT *AWOL*--

--WHILE JOHN KERRY *WENT* TO VIETNAM--AND WAS DECORATED *FIVE TIMES*--

--AND REPUBLICANS ARE TRYING TO MAKE AN ISSUE OUT OF *KERRY'S* RECORD?

YEP!

Panel 6:
I SEE I'VE GOT SOME CATCHING UP TO DO.

OH, DID I MENTION THAT *YOU'VE* BEEN A REPUBLICAN FOR THE LAST FIVE MONTHS?

VERY FUNNY. GO AWAY NOW.

TO BE CONTINUED...

TOM TOMORROW ©2004

THIS MODERN WORLD

by TOM TOMORROW

THE UNDECIDED VOTER

I'D *CONSIDER* VOTING FOR JOHN KERRY--BUT I JUST DON'T KNOW IF I TRUST HIM TO LEAD THE WAR ON *TERROR!*

OH REALLY?

ARE YOU WORRIED THAT HE MIGHT CYNICALLY EXPLOIT THE THREAT OF TERRORISM TO JUSTIFY THE IN-VASION OF A COUNTRY WHICH AC-TUALLY *POSES* NO THREAT-- DIVERTING OUR RESOURCES AND GIVING THE *REAL* TERRORISTS TIME TO *REGROUP?*

OR ARE YOU CONCERNED THAT THE COUNTRY IN QUESTION COULD BE-COME A BREEDING GROUND FOR *NEW* TERRORISTS AS A RESULT OF HIS *INCOMPETENT LEADER-SHIP*--LEAVING US MORE VULNER-ABLE THAN *BEFORE?*

OR ARE YOU JUST AFRAID THAT IN THE MIDDLE OF ALL THIS, HE'D BE SO INSANELY IRRESPONSIBLE AS TO RUN UP *RECORD DEFICITS* IN ORDER TO FINANCE A TAX CUT FOR THE WEALTHIEST *ONE PERCENT* OF THE *COUNTRY?*

WHAT *IS* IT, BIFF? WHAT IS IT ABOUT KERRY THAT *TROUBLES* YOU SO?

HE LOOKS *FRENCH.*

AND THERE'S THE *FLIP FLOPPING.*

AND STUFF.

I'M FILLED WITH CONFIDENCE, KNOW-ING THAT THIS ELECTION WILL BE DECIDED BY VOTERS LIKE YOU.

TOM TOMORROW©2004

THIS MODERN WORLD

by TOM TOMORROW

THE REPUBLICAN CONVENTIONEER'S GUIDE TO NEW YORK CITY

SURE, NEW YORK CITY IS FULL OF ATHEISTS, HOMOSEXUALS AND NEW YORK TIMES COLUMNISTS--BUT THAT DOESN'T MEAN REPUBLICANS WON'T BE *WELCOME* THERE!

WE WILL BE GREETED AS *LIBERATORS*--LIBERATING THEM FROM *LIBERALISM*!

THEY'LL BE TOO BUSY SHOWERING US WITH *ROSE PETALS* TO *PROTEST*!

WHY, THE *ESCORT SERVICES* ARE SAID TO BE BRINGING IN *EXTRA PROSTITUTES* FROM OUT OF TOWN TO MEET THE EXPECTED *DEMAND!**

LOOK--SOMETIMES A DELEGATE JUST NEEDS A *LEGITIMATE MASSAGE*!

ALL THAT CHEERING AND SIGN WAVING CAN *REALLY* STRAIN A PERSON'S BACK!

*TRUE.

AND, IF YOU NEED ANY MORE SURROGATES TO ATTACK KERRY, THERE ARE *PLENTY* OF HELPFUL NEW YORKERS WHO ARE *AT LEAST* AS CREDIBLE AS THE SWIFT BOAT VETS!

JOHN KERRY IS A *FLESH-EATING POD PERSON* FROM *JUPITER*! MY *FILLINGS* TOLD ME!

EXCUSE ME, I'M FROM *REGNERY*--WOULD YOU LIKE A *BOOK CONTRACT*?

OF COURSE, YOU'LL WANT TO FIND TIME TO VISIT THE WORLD TRADE CENTER SITE WHILE YOU'RE IN THE CITY! AFTER ALL--9/11 *BELONGS* TO YOU REPUBLICANS!

I'LL NEVER FORGET WHAT IT WAS LIKE TO WATCH THE TOWERS FALL OVER AND OVER AGAIN ON OUR LOCAL *FOX* AFFILIATE!

THESE LIBERAL NEW YORK ELITISTS CAN NEVER COMPREHEND WHAT *WE* WENT THROUGH THAT DAY!

AND, HEY--THERE'S EVEN AN *AIRCRAFT CARRIER* IN NEW YORK CITY*--IN CASE THE PRESIDENT WANTS TO PREMATURELY DECLARE *ANOTHER* MISSION "*ACCOMPLISHED*"...

HURRAY, I'M RE-ELECTED!

SIR, THE ELECTION IS TWO MONTHS AWAY.

MISSION ACCOMPLISH

HAVE YA *HEARD* OF DIEBOLD, KARL?

GOOD POINT, SIR! CONGRATULATIONS ON YOUR *VICTORY*!

*INTREPID SEA-AIR-SPACE MUSEUM, 46TH & 12TH.

TOM TOMORROW©2004

THIS MODERN WORLD

by TOM TOMORROW

ONCE AGAIN, IT'S TIME TO CHECK IN ON...
PARALLEL EARTH!

AS LONGTIME READERS WILL UNDOUBTEDLY RECALL, OUR INTER-DIMENSIONAL COUNTERPARTS HAD A LITTLE TROUBLE WITH *THEIR* LAST PRESIDENTIAL ELECTION TOO.

AND SO, DUE TO THIS PREVIOUSLY-UNNOTICED QUIRK IN OUR ELECTION LAWS, I MUST CONCEDE THE PRESIDENCY TO A *SMALL CUTE DOG!*

PARALLEL AL GORE

ARF!

NOW, ALMOST FOUR YEARS LATER, PARALLELIANS ARE *BITTERLY DIVIDED*...MANY STRONGLY SUPPORT THE PRESIDENT, NO MATTER *WHAT*--

HIS BRAIN MAY BE THE SIZE OF A *WALNUT*--BUT HE *IS* DECISIVE!

HE DOESN'T NEED A *FOCUS GROUP* TO TELL *HIM* WHAT TO PEE ON!

--WHILE MANY OTHERS *OPPOSE* HIM JUST AS *ADAMANTLY!*

LOOK, PARALLEL SENATOR KERRY MAY NOT BE THE MOST *CHARISMATIC* CANDIDATE WE'VE EVER SEEN--BUT AT LEAST HE IS ABLE TO SAY MORE THAN "ARF, ARF!"

AND HE HAS *OPPOSABLE THUMBS!*

ULTIMATELY, THE OUTCOME OF THE PARALLEL ELECTION MAY BE DETERMINED BY A HANDFUL OF *UNDECIDED VOTERS!*

DURING THE SMALL CUTE DOG'S PRESIDENCY, WE'VE HAD A TERRORIST ATTACK, SKYROCKETING DEFICITS AND A DISASTROUS WAR--

--BUT HOW DO WE KNOW HIS OPPONENT WON'T *REALLY* SCREW THINGS UP?

IN AN EFFORT TO *SWAY* THESE VOTERS, SUPPORTERS OF THE PRESIDENT HAVE BEEN ATTACKING PARALLEL KERRY'S *WAR RECORD.*

THEY HAVE INCONCLUSIVE EVIDENCE SUGGESTING THAT HE MAY NOT BE *QUITE* AS HEROIC AS HE HAS CLAIMED!

WELL THEN--*I'M* VOTIN' FOR THE *DOG!*

ASTONISHINGLY, IT HAS BECOME ONE OF THE BIGGEST CONTROVERSIES OF THE PARALLEL CAMPAIGN.

COMING UP NEXT: *IS* SENATOR KERRY QUALIFIED TO REPLACE A *SMALL CUTE DOG* WHOSE *BRAIN* IS NO BIGGER THAN A *WALNUT?* OUR EXPERTS *DEBATE* THE ISSUE!

BUT *FIRST*--FOOTAGE OF THE PRESIDENT POSING WITH *SOLDIERS* AND *FLAGS!*

Action McNews

WILL THE SMALL CUTE DOG *WIN?* STAY *TUNED!*

TOM TOMORROW©2004

103

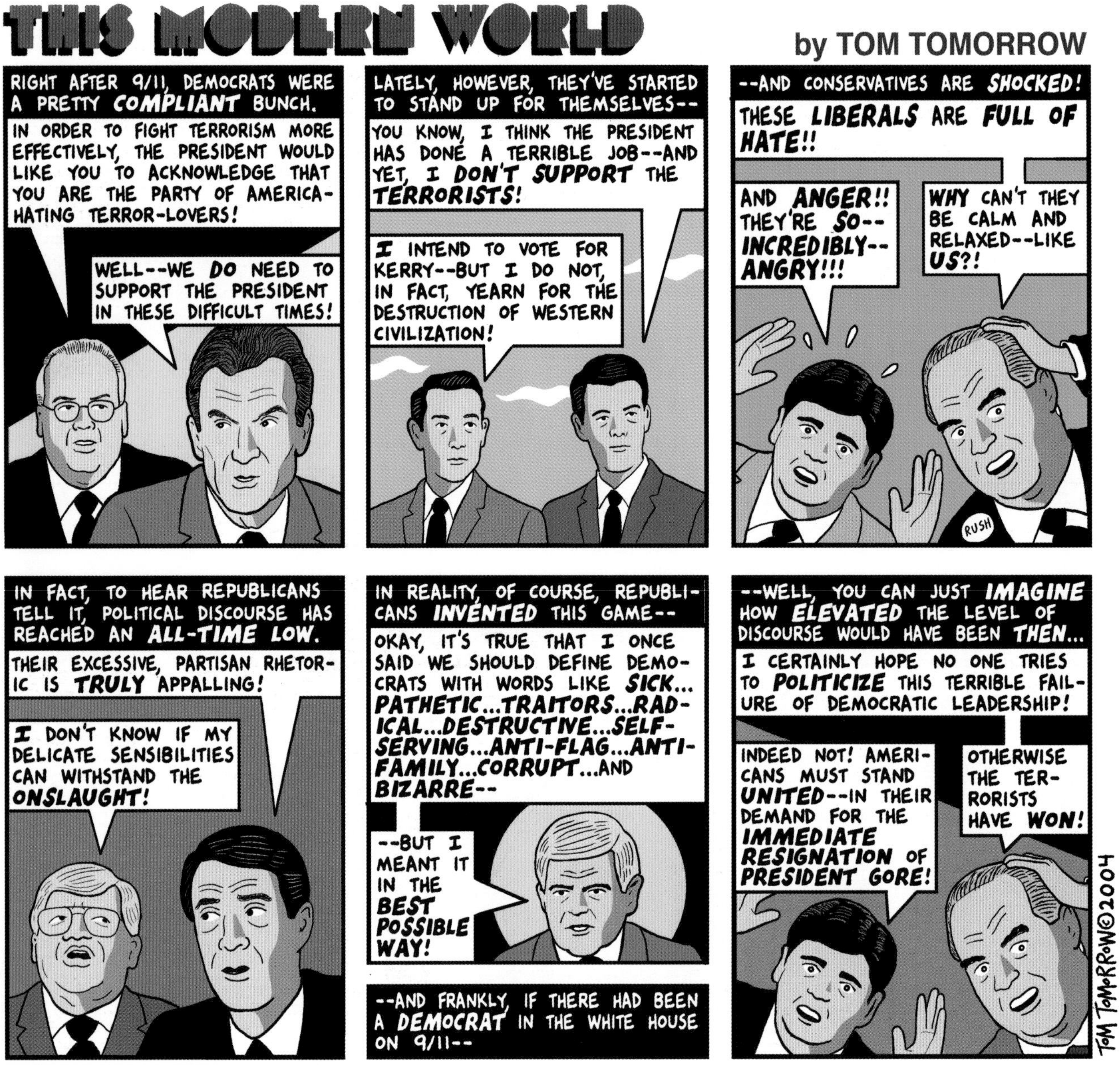
THIS MODERN WORLD
by TOM TOMORROW
RIGHT AFTER 9/11, DEMOCRATS WERE A PRETTY COMPLIANT BUNCH.
IN ORDER TO FIGHT TERRORISM MORE EFFECTIVELY, THE PRESIDENT WOULD LIKE YOU TO ACKNOWLEDGE THAT YOU ARE THE PARTY OF AMERICA-HATING TERROR-LOVERS!
WELL--WE DO NEED TO SUPPORT THE PRESIDENT IN THESE DIFFICULT TIMES!
LATELY, HOWEVER, THEY'VE STARTED TO STAND UP FOR THEMSELVES--
YOU KNOW, I THINK THE PRESIDENT HAS DONE A TERRIBLE JOB--AND YET, I DON'T SUPPORT THE TERRORISTS!
I INTEND TO VOTE FOR KERRY--BUT I DO NOT, IN FACT, YEARN FOR THE DESTRUCTION OF WESTERN CIVILIZATION!
--AND CONSERVATIVES ARE SHOCKED!
THESE LIBERALS ARE FULL OF HATE!!
AND ANGER!! THEY'RE SO--INCREDIBLY--ANGRY!!!
WHY CAN'T THEY BE CALM AND RELAXED--LIKE US?!
RUSH
IN FACT, TO HEAR REPUBLICANS TELL IT, POLITICAL DISCOURSE HAS REACHED AN ALL-TIME LOW.
THEIR EXCESSIVE, PARTISAN RHETORIC IS TRULY APPALLING!
I DON'T KNOW IF MY DELICATE SENSIBILITIES CAN WITHSTAND THE ONSLAUGHT!
IN REALITY, OF COURSE, REPUBLICANS INVENTED THIS GAME--
OKAY, IT'S TRUE THAT I ONCE SAID WE SHOULD DEFINE DEMOCRATS WITH WORDS LIKE SICK... PATHETIC...TRAITORS...RADICAL...DESTRUCTIVE...SELF-SERVING...ANTI-FLAG...ANTI-FAMILY...CORRUPT...AND BIZARRE--
--BUT I MEANT IT IN THE BEST POSSIBLE WAY!
--AND FRANKLY, IF THERE HAD BEEN A DEMOCRAT IN THE WHITE HOUSE ON 9/11--
--WELL, YOU CAN JUST IMAGINE HOW ELEVATED THE LEVEL OF DISCOURSE WOULD HAVE BEEN THEN...
I CERTAINLY HOPE NO ONE TRIES TO POLITICIZE THIS TERRIBLE FAILURE OF DEMOCRATIC LEADERSHIP!
INDEED NOT! AMERICANS MUST STAND UNITED--IN THEIR DEMAND FOR THE IMMEDIATE RESIGNATION OF PRESIDENT GORE!
OTHERWISE THE TERRORISTS HAVE WON!
TOM TOMORROW©2004

THIS MODERN WORLD

by TOM TOMORROW

EERIE PARALLELS

Panel 1:
JOHN KERRY IS EMBROILED IN A CONTROVERSY ABOUT HIS MILITARY SERVICE--

HE CLAIMS TO HAVE BEEN *VERY, VERY* HEROIC--BUT HE *MAY* HAVE BEEN MERELY *HEROIC!*

WELL THEN--HE'S LOST *MY* VOTE!

Panel 2:
--AND SO IS *GEORGE W. BUSH!*

THERE'S A *MOUNTAIN* OF EVIDENCE THAT HE PULLED STRINGS TO GET INTO THE NATIONAL GUARD--AND THEN WENT *AWOL*--

--BUT A *COUPLE* OF MEMOS MAY HAVE BEEN *FAKES!*

WELL THEN--WE *CLEARLY* NEED TO SPEND THE NEXT TWO MONTHS DISCUSSING THE MINUTIAE OF *TYPESETTING!*

Panel 3:
JOHN KERRY IS FREQUENTLY MISREPRESENTED IN THE MEDIA--

I WONDER WHAT THE FRENCH WORD FOR "FLIP FLOPPER" IS!

I DON'T KNOW--BUT I'LL BET *JOHN KERRY* DOES!

HA, HA!

HA, HA!

Panel 4:
--AND SO IS *GEORGE W. BUSH!*

NO DOUBT ABOUT IT, WANDA--THE *PRESIDENT* IS A MAN OF *QUIET STRENGTH* AND *STEADFAST RESOLVE!*

UNLIKE A CERTAIN FRENCH-SPEAKING *FLIP FLOPPER* I COULD NAME! HA, HA!

HA, HA!

Panel 5:
AND JOHN KERRY IS RUNNING AS THE CANDIDATE WHO CAN DO A BETTER JOB THAN GEORGE W. BUSH--

--SO YOU MIGHT AS *WELL* VOTE FOR ME! I MEAN--SERIOUSLY! HOW COULD I DO *WORSE?*

Panel 6:
--AND SO IS *GEORGE W. BUSH!*

I'VE GOT A PLAN TO *FIX* THIS ECONOMY! AND TO *WIN* THIS WAR!

VOTE FOR *ME*--AND I'LL CLEAN THIS MESS *UP!*

GEORGE, WE NEED TO HAVE A TALK.

NOT ONLY *THAT*--BUT KERRY HAS A *BUSH* IN HIS YARD--AND BUSH OFTEN *CARRIES* THINGS!

SPOOKY!

THIS MODERN WORLD

by TOM TOMORROW

CBS THINKS IT HAS A NEW ANGLE ON AN OLD STORY.

WE HAVE OBTAINED A **BAR TAB** RUN UP BY GEORGE W. BUSH IN 1967--**PROVING** THE PRESIDENT WAS ONCE A **DRUNKEN FRAT BOY!**

IT'S A **SCOOP**, I TELL YOU--A **SCOOP!!**

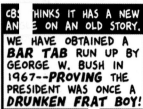

BUT **SOME GUY WITH A WEBSITE*** QUICKLY NOTES A **DISCREPANCY!**

SOMEONE HAS DOODLED A SEVENTIES-ERA "SMILEY FACE" ON ONE CORNER OF THE BAR TAB! **NO ONE** WAS DOODLING THE "SMILEY FACE" IN *1967!*

THIS BAR TAB IS A **FAKE!**

*"SOME GUY WITH A WEB-SITE" ©AUGUST POLLAK, WWW.XOVERBOARD.COM...

THE POSSIBILITY OF FOR-GERY SOON **DOMINATES** THE STORY!

UP NEXT, WE DEBATE THE **MOST IMPORTANT ISSUE** OF CAMPAIGN 2004--

--WHEN **DID** PEOPLE FIRST START DOODLING "SMILEY FACES"?

CBS IS ULTIMATELY FORCED TO ISSUE A RETRACTION.

THE DOCUMENT WAS FAXED TO US BY SOMEBODY WHO KNEW SOMEBODY WHO SAID HIS UNCLE USED TO BE A **BARTENDER!**

HOW WERE **WE** SUPPOSED TO KNOW IT WASN'T GENUINE?

THE WHITE HOUSE RESPONDS WITH **INDIGNATION!**

THERE ARE **QUESTIONS** WHICH NEED TO BE **ANSWERED!**

BY **CBS**, I MEAN! NOT BY **ME!**

NO UNANSWERED QUES-TIONS **HERE**, NOSIREE!

GO AWAY NOW.

GUYS WITH WEBSITES CAN'T STOP PATTING THEMSELVES ON THE BACK.

HAH! CBS MADE A **MIS-TAKE**--AND **WE CAUGHT THEM!** CAN THERE BE ANY DOUBT THAT THE **ENTIRE NEWS MEDIA** WILL SOON BE REPLACED BY **GUYS WITH WEB-SITES?**

I THINK **NOT.**

QUESTIONS ABOUT THE PRESIDENT'S PAST ARE APPARENTLY **FORGOTTEN.**

HECK--IF THAT BAR TAB WAS A **FORGERY,** IT CLEARLY PROVES THAT **NO** YALIE **EVER** DRANK TO EXCESS!

I THINK IT PROVES THAT THERE ARE **NO DRINKING ESTABLISHMENTS** IN **NEW HAVEN!**

AND SOMEWHERE, KARL ROVE SMILES.

GEE, KARL--THIS COULDN'T HAVE WORKED OUT BETTER IF YOU'D PLANTED THAT BAR TAB **YOURSELF!**

YES, WELL--WE MUSTN'T QUESTION OUR GOOD FOR-TUNE, SIR.

TOM TOMORROW©2004... www.thismodernworld.com

106

THIS MODERN WORLD

by TOM TOMORROW

IN THEIR OWN WORDS

"I BELIEVE DEMOLISHING HUSSEIN'S MILITARY POWER AND LIBERATING IRAQ WOULD BE A CAKEWALK."

--DEFENSE POLICY BOARD MEMBER KEN ADELMAN, 2/13/02.

"SIMPLY STATED, THERE IS NO DOUBT THAT SADDAM HUSSEIN NOW HAS WEAPONS OF MASS DESTRUCTION."

--VICE PRESIDENT DICK CHENEY, 8/26/02.

"WE DO KNOW THAT (SADDAM) IS ACTIVELY PURSUING A NUCLEAR WEAPON."

--NATIONAL SECURITY ADVISOR CONDOLEEZZA RICE, 9/10/02.

"IT IS NOT KNOWABLE HOW LONG THAT CONFLICT WOULD LAST. IT COULD LAST, YOU KNOW, SIX DAYS, SIX WEEKS. I DOUBT SIX MONTHS."

--SECRETARY OF DEFENSE DONALD RUMSFELD, 2/7/03.

"MY BELIEF IS WE WILL, IN FACT, BE GREETED AS LIBERATORS."

--CHENEY, 3/16/03.

"WE'RE DEALING WITH A COUNTRY THAT CAN REALLY FINANCE ITS OWN RECON-STRUCTION, AND RELATIVELY SOON."

--DEPUTY SECRETARY OF DEFENSE PAUL WOLFOWITZ, 3/27/03.

"WE KNOW WHERE (THE WEAPONS) ARE. THEY'RE IN THE AREA AROUND TIKRIT AND BAGHDAD AND EAST, WEST, NORTH AND SOUTH SOMEWHAT."

--RUMSFELD, 3/30/03.

"IRAQ WILL NOT REQUIRE SUSTAINED AID."

O.M.B. DIRECTOR MITCH DANIELS, 3/28/03.

"MAJOR COMBAT OPERA-TIONS HAVE ENDED."

--PRESIDENT GEORGE W. BUSH, 5/1/03.

"A YEAR FROM NOW I'D BE SURPRISED IF THERE'S NOT SOME GRAND SQUARE IN BAGHDAD THAT IS NAMED AFTER PRESIDENT BUSH."

--FORMER PENTAGON ADVISOR RICHARD PERLE, 9/22/03.

THE BUSH ADMINIS-TRATION: A TRACK RECORD THAT CAN'T BE DENIED

I'M GEORGE W. BUSH AND I DID **NOT** APPROVE THIS MESSAGE!

TOM TOMORROW©2004

THIS MODERN WORLD

by TOM TOMORROW

PARALLEL EARTH UPDATE: FOR FOUR YEARS, THE SMALL CUTE DOG'S HANDLERS HAVE KEPT HIM ON A *TIGHT LEASH*.

I'M SORRY--THE PRESIDENT DOESN'T HAVE TIME FOR *PRESS CONFERENCES*--

--HE'S TOO BUSY TAKING A *BITE* OUT OF *TERROR*!

PARALLEL SCOTT McCLELLAN

BUT AT THE FIRST *PARALLEL DEBATE*, NO SUCH PRECAUTIONS WERE *POSSIBLE*--

MR. PRESIDENT, WHY DO YOU FEEL YOU ARE MORE *QUALIFIED* THAN YOUR OPPONENT?

WHINE

WHIMPER

GRRRRRR

ARF!

--AND FRANKLY, THE PRESIDENT DIDN'T DO TOO WELL.

WILL SOMEBODY PLEASE ASK THE PRESIDENT TO STOP--ER--*LICKING HIMSELF*?

BAD DOGGIE! *BAD MR. PRESIDENT!* SIR!

(PARALLEL JOHN KERRY)

SLURP SLURP SLURP

FOR THE FIRST TIME IN *YEARS*, THE MEDIA SEEMED TO NOTICE THE *OBVIOUS*.

WHY--THE LEADER OF THE FREE PARALLEL WORLD IS NOTHING MORE THAN A *SMALL CUTE DOG*!

HE IS NOT VERY PRESIDENTIAL AT *ALL*!

WHY DIDN'T SOMEONE POINT THIS OUT *SOONER*?

Action McNews

PARALLEL DEMOCRATS FELT A RENEWED SENSE OF *OPTIMISM*.

WHY--THERE'S A *POSSIBILITY* THAT THE PUBLIC *MAY* CHOOSE THE CANDIDATE WHO ACTUALLY HAS *HIGHER COGNITIVE FUNCTIONS*!

MAYBE.

OF COURSE, THE PRESIDENT'S TEAM STILL HAD SEVERAL WEEKS TO *TURN THINGS AROUND*.

THE PRESIDENT MAY BE A SMALL CUTE DOG, CHRIS--BUT AT LEAST HE'S NOT A *FRENCH POODLE*!

HA, HA! *FRENCH!* THAT'S A *GOOD ONE*!

PARALLEL-- OH, YOU KNOW.

WILL THE CLEVER ONE-LINER WIN THE SMALL CUTE DOG A *SECOND TERM*? STAY *TUNED*!

TOM TOMORROW©2004

THIS MODERN WORLD

by TOM TOMORROW

OSAMA IS *VERY GOOD* AT MASTER-MINDING TERRORIST ATTACKS! THAT'S WHY WE *MUST* DEFEAT HIM!

CLICK!

--SO MY OPPONENT THINKS OSAMA IS "*VERY GOOD*"? WELL, *I* DON'T THINK OSAMA IS GOOD AT *ALL*! *I* THINK HE'S VERY *BAD*!

CLICK!

--JOHN KERRY IS ONE OF OSAMA'S *BIGGEST FANS*! HE THINKS OSAMA IS A *REALLY GREAT GUY*! THEY'RE PRACTICALLY *BEST FRIENDS*!

SNARL!

CLICK!

--BILL, I DON'T KNOW WHAT SEN-ATOR KERRY WAS *THINK-ING* WHEN HE PRAISED OSAMA BIN LADEN, BUT-

CLICK!

--IF JOHN KERRY LOVES OSAMA SO MUCH, WHY DON'T THEY JUST GO HAVE A *BIG GAY WEDDING*--IN *TAXACHUSSETTS*?! HAW, HAW!

CLICK!

--JOHN KERRY *CLAIMS* THAT THE PRESIDENT QUOTED HIM OUT OF CONTEXT! ED GILLESPIE--HOW DOES THE R.N.C. RESPOND TO THIS *ALLEGATION*?

WOLF, THE AMERICAN PEOPLE KNOW WHO THINKS OSAMA IS *GOOD*--AND WHO THINKS HE IS *BAD*!

CLICK!

--COMING UP NEXT: THE RESULTS OF OUR INTERNET POLL QUESTION-- DO *YOU* THINK OSAMA IS *GOOD*?

AND WE'LL FIND OUT IF JOHN KERRY *REALLY* THINKS OSAMA IS HIS *BEST FRIEND* IN THE *WHOLE WORLD*!

FIRST THESE MESSAGES!

CLICK!

TOM TOMORROW©2004

THIS MODERN WORLD

by TOM TOMORROW

UH--WHAT'S WITH THE *BLIND-FOLDS,* GUYS?

WHY--THESE ARE OUR *BLINDFOLDS FOR BUSH!*

THEY'RE HANDING THEM OUT *FREE* DOWN AT THE BUSH CAMPAIGN!

BUS STOP

YOU SEE, *REAL* AMERICANS ARE *SICK AND TIRED* OF WATCHING THE BIASED LIBERAL MEDIA TRY TO UNDERMINE OUR PRESIDENT--

--AND THANKS TO *BLINDFOLDS FOR BUSH,* WE NO LONGER *HAVE TO!*

BUS STOP

LET THEM BROADCAST THEIR BIASED *CASUALTY STATISTICS--WE* WON'T EVER SEE THEM! *LET* THEM SHOW THEIR BIASED *ABU GHRAIB PHOTOS--WE* WON'T BE LOOKING AT THEM!

WE'RE NOT GONNA SEE *ANYTHING* WE DON'T *WANT* TO SEE!

BUS STOP

YEP, *BLINDFOLDS FOR BUSH* MAY BE THE BEST THING TO HAPPEN TO THE REPUBLICAN PARTY SINCE *MONICA LEWINSKY!*

IF YOU SAY SO--

HEY!! WATCH OUT FOR THAT *BUS--*

BUS STOP

WHAM!!

YOU KNOW, I HAD A *FEELING* THIS WASN'T GOING TO END WELL...

SORRY, DID YOU SAY SOMETHING? I JUST PUT *FREEDOM PLUGS* IN MY EARS!

BUS STOP

"WE CREATE OUR OWN REALITY." --ANONYMOUS BUSH AIDE TO RON SUSKIND

TOM TOMORROW©2004

THIS MODERN WORLD

by TOM TOMORROW

DO-IT-YOURSELF FUNNIES

SPECIAL PRE-ELECTION DEADLINE EDITION!

INSTRUCTIONS: 1. CIRCLE THE OPTIONS WHICH MOST ACCURATELY REFLECT THE ACTUAL OUTCOME OF THE ELECTION. 2. GUFFAW HEARTILY.

GOSH, BIFF--THE OUTCOME OF **THIS** ELECTION DEFINITELY (is/is not) SUBJECT TO **DISPUTE!**

THAT'S **TRUE**, BETTY! (George Bush/John Kerry/neither man) WON AN **UNDENIABLY** (legitimate/questionable) VICTORY!

YES, IT IS CERTAINLY (fortunate/unfortunate) THAT THIS ELECTION (was not/was) MARRED BY VOTING IRREGULARITIES AS A RESULT OF (hacked voting machines/confusion and incompetence/outright fraud)!

THINGS DEFINITELY (could/could not) HAVE GONE WORSE!

OF COURSE, WE **CAN'T** FORGET THE EMOTIONS WE ALL FELT WHEN FEARS OF A LAST-MINUTE (terrorist attack/October Surprise/completely unpredictable event) TURNED OUT TO BE UTTERLY (prophetic/misguided)!

IT'S HARD TO **IMAGINE** HOW DIFFERENTLY THINGS MIGHT HAVE TURNED OUT IF IT (had/had not) REALLY **HAPPENED!**

AT **ANY** RATE--I'LL BET MOST AMERICANS ARE EXPERIENCING A SENSE OF (overwhelming relief/sickly despair) NOW THAT A REPEAT OF THE 2000 ELECTION DEBACLE (has been avoided/seems inevitable)!

WE SURE HAVE A LOT TO BE (grateful for/enraged by) **THIS** YEAR!

WE SURE **DO!** THIS ELECTION WAS **TRULY** PROOF THAT THE SYSTEM IS (in great shape/broken beyond any possibility of repair)!

I (could/couldn't) AGREE **MORE!**

THIS MODERN WORLD--THE CARTOON THAT'S ALWAYS TIMELY--EVEN WHEN IT'S **NOT!**

TOM TOMORROW©2004

THIS MODERN WORLD

by TOM TOMORROW

A FEW RANDOM REASONS GEORGE BUSH WAS NOT DEFEATED IN A LANDSLIDE

TOO MANY AMERICANS WERE UNTROUBLED BY THE ABU GHRAIB PHOTOS AND ALL THAT THEY IMPLIED.

THOSE WERE JUST THE HARMLESS FRATERNITY-STYLE *HIJINKS* OF A *FEW BAD APPLES!*

I PREFER TO THINK OF THEM AS *MISGUIDED* APPLES!

TOO MANY AMERICANS BELIEVED SADDAM DID HAVE WMD'S, AND/OR WAS RESPONSIBLE FOR 9/11.

IF WE HADN'T ACTED WHEN WE DID, AMERICA MIGHT BE NOTHING MORE THAN A PILE OF RADIOACTIVE *RUBBLE* BY NOW!

I FEEL LIKE I'M GOING TO HAVE A HEADACHE FOR THE NEXT FOUR YEARS.

TOO MANY AMERICANS BELIEVED THAT JOHN KERRY WOULD NOT HAVE TAKEN THE WAR ON TERROR SERIOUSLY ENOUGH.

SIR, WE'VE GOT OSAMA *PINPOINTED*--

NOT *NOW!* CAN'T YOU SEE THAT KEN AND BARBIE ARE ABOUT TO GO ON A *DATE?*

YOU LOOK VERY FETCHING TONIGHT BARBIE!

WHY THANK YOU KEN!

TOO MANY AMERICANS AGREED THAT GAY MARRIAGE POSES AN IMMINENT THREAT TO SOCIETY.

I DON'T CARE ABOUT JOBS OR HEALTH CARE OR *ANY* OF THAT DEMOCRAT NONSENSE--

--THE *IMPORTANT* THING IS THAT HOMOS CAN'T GET *MARRIED!*

AND TOO MANY AMERICANS *DISAGREED* WITH BUSH ON SOCIAL ISSUES--BUT VOTED FOR HIM ANYWAY.

I *REALLY* WANT ANOTHER $300 TAX REBATE!

I'M SURE THE SCALIA COURT WON'T BE *THAT* BAD!

TOM TOMORROW©2004

THIS MODERN WORLD

by TOM TOMORROW

THIS MODERN WORLD

by TOM TOMORROW

THINGS TO BE THANKFUL FOR THIS HOLIDAY SEASON

1) THE NEXT PRESIDENTIAL ELECTION IS A SCANT **FOUR YEARS** AWAY!

THAT'S A MERE 1,460 DAYS, GIVE OR TAKE!

OR, IF YOU PREFER, 35,040 **HOURS!**

BUT HEY, WHO'S COUNTING?

2) SOME TATTERED SHREDS OF OUR DEMOCRACY **MAY** ACTUALLY SURVIVE UNTIL ELECTION DAY 2008!

YOU HAVE THE RIGHT TO VOTE REPUBLICAN. IF YOU CHOOSE NOT TO VOTE REPUBLICAN, THE MACHINE WILL DO IT FOR YOU.

? ...

DIEBOLD
choose one:
☐ REPUBL
☐ REPUB

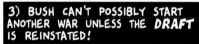

3) BUSH CAN'T POSSIBLY START ANOTHER WAR UNLESS THE **DRAFT** IS REINSTATED!

AND HE **PROMISED** THAT WASN'T GOING TO HAPPEN!

WELL, THEN! WE'VE CLEARLY GOT **NOTHING** TO **WORRY ABOUT!**

4) WITHOUT A TIME MACHINE, HE WON'T **LITERALLY** BE ABLE TO APPOINT ANY NEANDERTHALS TO THE SUPREME COURT!

UGG NOT **CARE** ABOUT CIVIL RIGHTS! UGG SAY SMASH CRIMINALS WITH **BIG ROCK!**

OOG DISSENT! OOG SAY SMASH WITH **TWO** BIG ROCKS!

VERY SOUND JUDICIAL REASONING.

5) REPUBLICANS CAN'T ENACT THEIR EXTREMIST AGENDA **OVERNIGHT!**

HECK, NO! IN ORDER TO DESTROY WHAT'S LEFT OF THE SOCIAL SAFETY NET--

--**AND** PERMANENTLY TILT THE TAX CODE IN FAVOR OF THE RICH--

--THEY'LL NEED AT **LEAST** A COUPLE OF **MONTHS!**

SO HAPPY THANKSGIVING!

TOM TOMORROW©2004

THIS MODERN WORLD

by TOM TOMORROW

OKAY, LOOK...WE KNOW HOW THIS IS GOING TO PLAY OUT...

WE'LL HAVE THE DIRE *WARNINGS*...

IRAN IS *HOURS* AWAY FROM PERFECTING REALLY, *REALLY* TERRIBLE WEAPONS WHICH COULD BE USED ON *YOUR DEFENSELESS CHILDREN!*

AND THIS TIME WE'RE *SERIOUS!*

...THE FLIMSY *EVIDENCE*...

THIS IMAGE *CLEARLY* SHOWS AYATOLLAH KHAMENEI MEETING WITH OSAMA BIN LADEN AT A PRAGUE CAFE!

CAN'T YOU *SEE* IT?

I THINK IT LOOKS LIKE A *BUNNY RABBIT!*

HE MOUNTING PUBLIC *HYSTERIA*...

OH MY *GOD!* THE IRANIANS ARE GOING TO *GET* US! THEY'RE GOING TO GET US *ALL!*

WILL WE *EVER* FEEL SAFE *AGAIN*--LIKE WE DID DURING THE *COLD WAR*??

...AND OF COURSE, THE COMPLIANT *MEDIA.*

ARE THESE TODAY'S TALKING POINTS? GOLLY, THEY SURE *ARE!* WOULD I LIKE YOU ALL TO REPRINT THEM VERBATIM? YOU *BET* I WOULD!

NO PROBLEMO!

WE'RE HAPPY TO HELP!

Blah blah blah.
Blah blah blah bl...
Blah blah bl...

SO MAYBE WE SHOULD JUST SAVE EVERYONE A LOT OF TROUBLE AND SKIP AHEAD DIRECTLY TO THE *QUAGMIRE.*

YOU'RE MAKING ONE OF YOUR LITTLE *POINTS* AGAIN, AREN'T YOU?

TOM TOMORROW©2004

THIS MODERN WORLD

by TOM TOMORROW

THE GREAT DEBATE

CAN'T WE JUST BE **FRIENDS**?

PREPARE TO MEET YOUR **DOOM**!

left VS. **right**

1) DEMOCRATS, CHASTENED AFTER LOSING BY A NARROW MARGIN, DECIDE THEY MUST FIND COMMON GROUND WITH CONSERVATIVE VOTERS.

MANY LIBERALS HAVE RELIGIOUS VALUES **TOO**--IN A SECULAR, NONJUDGMENTAL KIND OF WAY, OF COURSE!

YOU SEE? WE ARE **NOT** SO VERY DIFFERENT FROM YOU!

2) REPUBLICANS, EXHILARATED AFTER WINNING BY A NARROW MARGIN, CONTINUE TO DEMONIZE APPROXIMATELY HALF THE VOTING POPULATION.

THEY'RE NOT **ANYTHING** LIKE US! WHY, I'M NOT COMPLETELY SURE THEY'RE EVEN **HUMAN**!

FOR ALL **WE** KNOW, THEY MIGHT BE **SPACE ALIENS**-- OR **EVIL ROBOTS** FROM THE **FUTURE**!

3) THE NEWS MEDIA, BENDING OVER BACKWARDS TO AVOID ACCUSATIONS OF LIBERAL BIAS, TREAT THE LATEST REPUBLICAN CHARGES WITH CAREFUL IMPARTIALITY.

PROFESSOR, IS IT **POSSIBLE** THAT DEMOCRATS **ARE** ACTUALLY ALIENS-- OR, UH, ROBOTS--**POSING** AS HUMANS?

ABSOLUTELY! WITH SUFFICIENTLY ADVANCED TECHNOLOGY, **ANYTHING** IS POSSIBLE!

4) DEMOCRATS, ONCE AGAIN, FIND THEMSELVES PLAYING DEFENSE.

WE'RE JUST AS HUMAN AS ANY REPUBLICAN--AND WE'LL SUBMIT TO **ANY** INVASIVE, HUMILIATING MEDICAL PROCEDURE NECESSARY TO **PROVE** IT!

AND THEN, WE'RE SORT OF HOPING THE PRESIDENT WILL **REPUDIATE** THIS DARN RUMOR. IF IT'S NOT TOO MUCH TROUBLE.

5) AND BEFORE ANYONE HAS TIME TO BLINK, REPUBLICANS INITIATE A NEW LINE OF ATTACK.

THIS **SHOCKING** DEMOCRAT DEMAND FOR **SPECIAL TREATMENT** FROM THE **PRESIDENT** CONFIRMS THEIR **FUNDAMENTAL DISRESPECT** FOR THE PRINCIPLES UPON WHICH THIS COUNTRY WAS **FOUNDED**!

JUST WHAT YOU'D **EXPECT** FROM A BUNCH OF AMERICA-HATING ROBOTS AND/OR ALIENS!

6) SEQUENCE REPEATS (WITH MINOR VARIATIONS) AD NAUSEUM.

TOM TOMORROW©2004

THIS MODERN WORLD

by TOM TOMORROW

THE PROBLEM: CONSERVATIVES ARE FLUSH WITH *VICTORY*--

HAH! WE CONTROL *EVERYTHING*! *NO ONE* CARES WHAT *LIBERALS* THINK ANYMORE!

EXCEPT OTHER LIBERALS!

AND WHO CARES ABOUT *THEM*?

--BUT THEY STILL WANT TO PRESENT THEMSELVES AS *VICTIMS*.

OF COURSE, WE HAVE NOT ELIMINATED THE SCOURGE OF *PERVASIVE LIBERAL BIAS*!

TRULY, OUR STRUGGLE NEVER *ENDS*!

HOW WE FIND THE STRENGTH TO CARRY ON, I'LL NEVER KNOW!

THE SOLUTION: PRETEND THAT SOMEONE WITH NO POWER WHATSOEVER IS ACTUALLY *VERY* POWERFUL--

FOR INSTANCE, LET'S NOT FORGET ABOUT ALL THE LEFT WING *COLLEGE PROFESSORS*!

THEY'RE TEACHING THE NEXT GENERATION TO *HATE AMERICA*!

SOMETHING MUST BE *DONE*!

--AND FIGHT WITH RENEWED VIGOR UNTIL YET ANOTHER BATTLE IS *WON*!

HAH! WE SURE TAUGHT THOSE SMARTYPANTS *PROFESSORS* A LESSON!

IF THEY DON'T WANT TO SIGN THE NEW, MANDATORY *LOYALTY OATH*--

--LET 'EM TEACH IN *CANADA*! HAW, HAW!

YEP.

WELL.

OKAY, THEN.

THE PROBLEM: WHO TO GO AFTER *NEXT*.

THIS BOOKSTORE CLERK GAVE ME A *REALLY DISDAINFUL LOOK* WHEN I BOUGHT ANN COULTER'S LATEST BESTSELLER!

YOU MEAN THE ISLAMOFASCISTS HAVE EVEN INFILTRATED OUR *BOOKSTORES*??

GENTLEMEN, I BELIEVE WE HAVE A *JOB* TO DO!

TOM TOMORROW©2004

117

THIS MODERN WORLD

by TOM TOMORROW

IT'S THE HEARTWARMING ANIMATED SPECIAL...

HOW THE FOX NEWS TEAM SAVED CHRISTMAS!

NOW ON DVD!

A RANKIN BASS PRODUCTION

WATCH THE *REAL* HEROES OF THE CHRISTMAS SEASON!

YOU WANNA KNOW WHO'S WATCHING OUT FOR *CHRISTMAS*? *ME! BILL O'REILLY! I'M* WATCHING OUT FOR CHRISTMAS!

SOMEBODY'S GOTTA DO IT!

?

SEE THEM STRUGGLE AGAINST THE CHRISTMAS-HATING FORCES OF *POLITICAL CORRECTNESS!*

YOU SECULAR HUMANISTS DON'T *WANT* US TO DECORATE OUR CHRISTMAS TREES--OR TELL OUR CHILDREN ABOUT SANTA--*DO YOU?!?*

ER--I--

DESTINED TO BECOME A *HOLIDAY CLASSIC!*

HEY! DON'T YOU MEAN A *CHRISTMAS* CLASSIC?!

MAN! IF IT WEREN'T FOR *US*, THERE WOULDN'T *BE A* CHRISTMAS!

AND BY "US," I MEAN "ME."

TOM TOMORROW©2004

118

THIS MODERN WORLD

by TOM TOMORROW

1) RUMSFELD MAKES A REVEALINGLY CALLOUS REMARK.

"--YOU CAN HAVE ALL THE ARMOR IN THE WORLD ON A TANK AND THE TANK CAN STILL BE BLOWN UP!"

2) THE SPIN MACHINE LEAPS INTO ACTION.

--AND SINCE THERE ARE *SOME SITUATIONS* IN WHICH ARMOR IS INEFFECTIVE--

--THERE IS CLEARLY *NO NEED* FOR ANY MORE ARMOR!

CLICK!

--THE TROOPS GET WHAT THEY NEED FROM JUNK PILES! THEY'RE *RECYCLING!* YOU'D THINK THE LIBERALS WOULD BE *HAPPY!*

SHEESH! THERE'S JUST *NO PLEASING* THE LIBERALS!

CLICK!

--IT'S NOT THE LACK OF *ARMOR* OR INDEFINITE *DEPLOYMENTS* THAT HURT MORALE--IT'S THE PEOPLE WHO DRAW *ATTENTION* TO THE LACK OF ARMOR AND INDEFINITE DEPLOYMENTS THAT HURT MORALE!

THEY MUST *REALLY* HATE THE TROOPS!

CLICK!

--THE QUESTION WAS PLANTED BY A *REPORTER,* ANYWAY!

I'LL BET HE ENGINEERED THE SPONTANEOUS ROAR OF *APPLAUSE,* AS WELL!

3) ACROSS THE COUNTRY, REPUBLICAN HEADS EXPLODE.

MUST-- SUPPORT-- TROOPS-- YAAUGH!

BUT-- MUST-- SUPPORT-- RUMMY-- AAIEEE!

MUST-- BLAME-- LIBERAL-- MEDIA-- YAARGH!

BOOM! *BOOM!* *BOOM!*

119

THIS MODERN WORLD

by TOM TOMORROW

1) DETERMINED IDEOLOGUES SPEND YEARS QUIETLY LAYING THE GROUNDWORK.

--SO YOU SEE, WHAT WE *REALLY* NEED TO DO IS--

--INVADE IRAQ!!

Project for the New American Century

--PRIVATIZE SOCIAL SECURITY!!

Cato Institute

2) A POLITICALLY SYMPATHETIC ADMINISTRATION RATCHETS UP THE RHETORIC.

THE IMPENDING THREAT POSED BY SADDAM'S WMD'S--

THE IMPENDING COLLAPSE OF THE SOCIAL SECURITY SYSTEM--

--MUST BE DEALT WITH!!

3) A STEADY DIET OF LIES AND MISINFORMATION FEEDS A GROWING PUBLIC HYSTERIA.

OH MY *GOD!* WE'VE GOT TO DO *SOMETHING*-- WHILE THERE'S STILL *TIME* TO SAVE--

--OUR NATION FROM *SADDAM!!*

--SOCIAL SECURITY FROM *BANKRUPTCY!!*

4) AN UTTERLY PREDICTABLE OUTCOME CATCHES EVERY-ONE OFF GUARD.

WHO COULD HAVE *POSSIBLY* FORESEEN THAT--

--THE IRAQ WAR--

--SOCIAL SECURITY RE-FORM--

--WOULD TURN INTO SUCH A *DEBACLE*?!?

TOM TOMORROW©2005

THIS MODERN WORLD

by TOM TOMORROW

THIS WEEK: HOW TO ARGUE LIKE A RIGHT WING PUNDIT

1) PRESENT WISHFUL THINKING AS OBJECTIVE REALITY.

--EVERYONE KNOWS THAT "VALUES VOTERS" GAVE PRESIDENT BUSH AN OVERWHELMING MANDATE!

EVEN A LIBERAL LIKE YOU HAS TO ACKNOWLEDGE THAT!

ER--UH--

2) INVOKE THE FOUNDING FATHERS WHENEVER POSSIBLE.

--THE FOUNDING FATHERS CERTAINLY DID NOT INTEND FOR DEMOCRATS TO QUESTION ALBERTO GONZALES ABOUT THOSE TORTURE MEMOS!

THE FOUNDING FATHERS FORESAW A NATION IN WHICH GONZALES WOULD SAIL THROUGH HIS CONFIRMATION!

ER--UH--

3) BE DELIBERATELY OBTUSE.

--SO SOME U.N. OFFICIAL THINKS THE AMERICAN GOVERNMENT IS "STINGY" WITH FOREIGN AID?

WELL, A GIRL SCOUT TROOP IN BILOXI, MISSISSIPPI RAISED FIVE THOUSAND DOLLARS FOR TSUNAMI RELIEF!

DOESN'T SOUND VERY "STINGY" TO ME!

ER--UH--

4) NEVER MISS AN OPPORTUNITY TO PUSH YOUR AGENDA.

SPEAKING OF TSUNAMI RELIEF--THIS TRAGEDY CLEARLY HIGHLIGHTS THE NEED TO REFORM THE SOCIAL SECURITY SYSTEM--

--BEFORE IT IS WIPED OUT--BY A FINANCIAL TSUNAMI!

ER--UH--

5) NEVER ADMIT YOU HAVE AN AGENDA.

--LOOK, I'M JUST TRYING TO HAVE A REASONABLE DISCUSSION ABOUT THE NEED FOR INTERMENT CAMPS!

CAN I HELP IT IF MISTER "LOONEY LEFT" HERE IS HAVING A TOTAL MELTDOWN?

ER--UH--

SHEESH! CALM DOWN BEFORE YOU HAVE A STROKE!

TOM TOMORROW©2005

THIS MODERN WORLD

by TOM TOMORROW

THE PRESIDENT IS REPORTEDLY A **SELECTIVE** LISTENER.

SIR, ANOTHER **CAR BOMB** HAS EXPLODED--

AND DID IT THEN PROCEED TO SHOWER OUR TROOPS WITH A GENTLE CLOUD OF **ROSE PETALS**, MAYHAP?

ER--NO, SIR, IT DID NOT--

THEN **BEGONE!** I DO NOT WISH TO BE **BOTHERED** WITH SUCH **TRIFLES!**

A LOT OF REPUBLICANS TRY TO FOLLOW HIS EXAMPLE... IGNORING, FOR INSTANCE, **ANY** EVIDENCE OF U.S. TORTURE BEYOND THE ABU GHRAIB PHOTOS...

BUT--WHAT ABOUT THE TAGUBA REPORT? DETAINEES SODOMIZED WITH LIGHTSTICKS? WATERBOARDING AT GITMO? DOCUMENTED DETAINEE **DEATHS**? THE RED CROSS REPORT? FBI AGENTS EXPRESSING CONCERN AS FAR BACK AS 2002? AND ON AND ON--

LA LA LA LA LA LA! I CAN'T **HEAAARRR** YOU!!

YOU CAN CERTAINLY EXPECT MORE OF THE SAME IF THE PENTAGON DECIDES TO PURSUE WHAT IT CALLS THE "SALVADOR OPTION" IN IRAQ...

AS IN **EL SALVADOR**, DURING THE EIGHTIES...YOU KNOW--DEATH SQUADS, MASSACRES, ASSASSINATIONS, KIDNAPPING...THAT SORT OF THING...

CAN'T HEAR A WORD YOU'RE **SAAAYIIIING!** LA LA LA LA LA LA LA LA LA!

FOR THAT MATTER, THERE'S REALLY NO TELLING **WHAT** LOYAL REPUBLICANS WILL HAVE TO IGNORE OVER THE NEXT FOUR YEARS...

DID YOU HEAR THAT **CIVIL LIBERTIES** HAVE BEEN SUSPENDED AND **MARTIAL LAW** DECLARED?

I BELIEVE YOU MEAN TO SAY THAT **TERROR CODDLING** HAS BEEN SUSPENDED AND **FREEDOM GUIDELINES** HAVE BEEN ISSUED.

UH--**RIGHT!** THAT'S WHAT I GET FOR LISTENING TO THE **BIASED LIBERAL MEDIA!**

PLEASE DON'T REPORT ME.

TOM TOMORROW©2005

THIS MODERN WORLD

by TOM TOMORROW

HOW LOW CAN WE GO?

THE DISTURBINGLY BRIEF JOURNEY FROM UNTHINKABLE TO MUNDANE

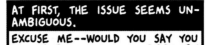

AT FIRST, THE ISSUE SEEMS UNAMBIGUOUS.

EXCUSE ME--WOULD YOU SAY YOU ARE *FOR* TORTURE--OR *AGAINST* IT?

OH, *DEFINITELY* "AGAINST"!

NO QUESTION *ABOUT* IT!

BUT UNFORTUNATE REVELATIONS FORCE MANY CONSERVATIVES TO ADOPT A MORE *NUANCED* STANCE.

I DON'T KNOW IF YOU CAN REALLY DEFINE SODOMY WITH A LIGHTSTICK AS *TORTURE*!

IT SOUNDS LIKE ANOTHER HARMLESS *FRATERNITY PRANK* TO *ME*!

REASONABLE PEOPLE FIND THEMSELVES DEBATING THINGS WHICH REALLY SHOULD NOT BE SUBJECT TO DEBATE.

I JUST DON'T THINK SODOMY WITH LIGHTSTICKS REFLECTS WELL ON US AS A NATION!

WHAT--DOES IT FAIL A "GLOBAL TEST"?

SNICKER! ARE YOU AFRAID THE *SURRENDER MONKEYS* WILL DISAPPROVE?

EVENTUALLY IT BECOMES AN ACT OF SINGULAR COURAGE FOR A CONSERVATIVE TO STATE THE OBVIOUS.

I MAY BE GOING WAY OUT ON A *LIMB* HERE--BUT GOSH DARN IT, TORTURE IS *WRONG*!

OH, LISTEN TO *MICHAEL MOORE JUNIOR*, HERE!

BEEN READING *MARX* AND *ENGELS* AGAIN, HAVE YOU?

AND THE BAR IS LOWERED JUST A LITTLE BIT FURTHER FOR NEXT TIME.

I THINK WE SHOULD STRAP DETAINEES DOWN AND FORCE THEM TO EAT THEIR *OWN LIVERS*!

HEY--WHATEVER IT *TAKES*... TO DEFEND OUR *FUNDAMENTAL AMERICAN VALUES*!!

TOM TOMORROW©2005

THIS MODERN WORLD

by TOM TOMORROW

HEY KIDS! IT'S --

MISTER McBOBO

THE INTELLEC-TUALLY NEARSIGHTED PUNDIT!

YOU'LL CHUCKLE AT HIS ZANY ANTICS AS HE MIS-INTERPRETS *EVERYTHING HE SEES!*

HO THERE! IT'S A TYPICAL *RED STATE DINING ESTABLISHMENT!* WHY, I BET YOU COULD NOT SPEND $20 ON A MEAL HERE IF YOU *TRIED!*

JOE'S HARDWARE

WELL, THAT'S ENOUGH RESEARCH FOR ONE DAY--I'VE GOT A *COLUMN* TO WRITE!

YOU'LL QUAKE WITH MIRTH AS HE EXPLAINS ANOTHER OF HIS *WACKY SOCIOLOGICAL THEORIES!*

YOU SEE, LADIES, *I* BELIEVE IT WOULD BE LOGICAL FOR YOU TO MARRY AS *EARLY AS POSSIBLE*--DEVOTE YOUR TIME TO *RAISING BABIES*--AND THEN START YOUR *CAREERS* AT THE AGE OF *FORTY!*

HECK, WE'LL EVEN THROW IN A *TAX CUT* SO YOU CAN BUY YOURSELVES SOMETHING *NICE!*

EXIT

AND YOU'LL GASP IN ASTONISHMENT AS HE FILLS ENDLESS COLUMN INCHES WITH THE MOST ACHINGLY BANAL OBSERVATIONS *IMAGINABLE!*

IN *RED STATES*, PEOPLE USE *LEAF BLOWERS!*

IN *BLUE STATES*, PEOPLE SIP *CHAR-DONNAY!*

RED STATERS ARE FILLED WITH *VIR-TUOUS JOY!*

BLUE STATERS NEED TO TURN THEIR *FROWNS UPSIDE DOWN!*

IT'S ALL *SO SIMPLE*--WHEN YOU SEE THINGS AS CLEARLY AS *I* DO!

TOM TOMORROW©2005

THIS MODERN WORLD

by TOM TOMORROW

APRIL 9, 2003: VICTORY SEEMS *IMMINENT* AFTER A BIG STATUE OF SADDAM IS TOPPLED.

WE'VE CERTAINLY TURNED THE CORNER *NOW!*

IRAQ WILL BE FREE AND STABLE BEFORE WE *KNOW* IT!

MAY 1, 2003: VICTORY SEEMS *IMMINENT* AFTER PRESIDENT BUSH DECLARES MAJOR COMBAT OPERATIONS OVER.

OKAY, WE'VE *REALLY* TURNED THE CORNER THIS TIME!

THE PROXIMITY OF A FREE AND STABLE IRAQ GROWS *EVER NEARER!*

DECEMBER 13, 2003: VICTORY SEEMS *IMMINENT* AFTER SADDAM IS PULLED OUT OF A HOLE IN THE GROUND.

THIS IS THE MOTHER OF *ALL CORNERS*--AND WE ARE *TURNING IT!*

THOSE WHO DO NOT FAVOR FREEDOM AND STABILITY WILL SOON BE *VERY DISAPPOINTED!*

JUNE 28, 2004: VICTORY SEEMS *IMMINENT* AFTER THE U.S. HANDS OVER LIMITED SOVEREIGNTY.

IF THIS DOES NOT CONSTITUTE THE TURNING OF A CORNER, I SIMPLY DON'T KNOW WHAT *DOES!*

WHY CAN'T LIBERALS *ACKNOWLEDGE* THE FREEDOM AND STABILITY TOWARD WHICH WE ARE INEVITABLY HEADED?

JANUARY 30, 2005: VICTORY SEEMS *IMMINENT* AFTER ELECTIONS ARE HELD WITHOUT MAJOR DISRUPTION.

A LIST OF CORNERS WE HAVE *NOT* TURNED WOULD SURELY NOT INCLUDE *THIS* ONE!

A FREE AND STABLE IRAQ IS SO CLOSE I CAN *TASTE* IT! AND IT TASTES *FREE*-- AND *STABLE!*

MAY 5, 2012: VICTORY SEEMS *IMMINENT* AFTER YET ANOTHER CORNER IS TURNED.

AND NOW THAT WE HAVE TURNED *THAT* CORNER, WE'VE *DEFINITELY* TURNED THE CORNER!

FREEDOM AND STABILITY ARE WAITING PATIENTLY--*JUST AROUND THE CORNER!*

TOM TOMORROW©2005

125

THIS MODERN WORLD

by TOM TOMORROW

Panel 1:
YOU'RE ABOUT TO ENTER A WORLD WHERE REALITY AND FANTASY *COLLIDE*...WHERE LOGIC HOLDS NO SWAY AND NUMBERS HAVE NO *MEANING*...YOU'RE ENTERING--

The REPUBLICAN ZONE

$E=mc^3$

DEE DEE DEE DEE

Panel 2:
PRESENTED FOR YOUR CONSIDERATION: STRANGE BEINGS WHO SAY THEY ONLY WANT TO *HELP*...

WE ARE THE *CONSERVATROIDS!* WE HAVE COME TO WARN YOU THAT YOUR PRIMITIVE SOCIAL SECURITY SYSTEM WILL *COLLAPSE* IN FORTY OF YOUR *EARTH YEARS*--

--UNLESS YOU FOLLOW *OUR* ADVICE!

SERVING ELDERLY HUMANS

Panel 3:
AVERAGE CITIZENS TRY TO MAKE SENSE OF IT ALL!

IF NOT FOR THE SUPERIOR INTELLECT OF THE *CONSERVATROIDS*, WE MIGHT NOT EVEN HAVE *KNOWN* THAT SOCIAL SECURITY IS FACING SUCH A CRISIS!

WE'RE LUCKY THESE ADVANCED BEINGS ARE WILLING TO SHARE THE WISDOM OF THEIR ADVANCED *THINK TANKS!*

The Daily Times
CONSERVATROIDS PROMISE NEW ERA

Panel 4:
SOON, THE HEAD CONSERVATROID ADDRESSES A JOINT SESSION OF CONGRESS!

--AND SO, UNDER *OUR* PLAN, EARTHLINGS WILL EXERT GREATER CONTROL OVER THEIR ACCUMULATED UNITS OF EXCHANGE!

THANK YOU, AND MAY THE DEITY YOU SO PRIMITIVELY WORSHIP BE PERCEIVED AS TREATING *YOUR* NATION-STATE WITH FAVORITISM!

HE ACCIDENTALLY LEAVES HIS BOOK *BEHIND!*

SERVING ELDERLY HUMANS

Panel 5:
ECONOMISTS STRUGGLE TO DECIPHER THE CONSERVATROID PROPOSAL!

THESE NUMBERS JUST DON'T ADD UP! IT *LOOKS* AS THOUGH THEY WANT TO SPEND 4.5 TRILLION DOLLARS *MORE* ON A SYSTEM WHICH WILL EVENTUALLY PROVIDE *SMALLER BENEFITS!*

THAT MAKES NO SENSE WHATSOEVER! WE MUST BE *MISSING* SOMETHING!

Panel 6:
FINALLY--THE SHOCKING *TWIST ENDING!*

I FINISHED THE TRANSLATION! THIS ISN'T A PLAN TO REFORM SOCIAL SECURITY AT *ALL!* IT'S--IT'S--

--IT'S A COOKBOOK!!

WOW! I *TOTALLY* DID NOT SEE *THAT* COMING!

SERVING ELDERLY HUMANS FOR DINNER

TOM TOMORROW©2005

THIS MODERN WORLD

by TOM TOMORROW

FURTHER WAYS TO ARGUE LIKE A CONSER-VATIVE

A SADLY ONGOING SERIES

1) USE ANY TENUOUS EXCUSE TO SEIZE THE MORAL HIGH GROUND.

I JUST DON'T KNOW IF ALBERTO GONZALES SHOULD REALLY BE ATTORNEY GENERAL AFTER WRITING THOSE *TORTURE MEMOS*--

I THINK YOU'RE JUST A *RACIST*.

ER--SAY *WHAT*--?

SILENCE! I'LL HEAR NO MORE OF YOUR *BIGOTED RAVINGS*!

2) CONCEDE NOTHING.

ANYWAY, THERE WAS *NO TORTURE!*

BUT--BUT--THE *EVIDENCE*--

I HAVEN'T SEEN ANY OF THIS SO-CALLED "EVIDENCE"! I THINK YOU'RE MAKING THE *WHOLE THING UP!*

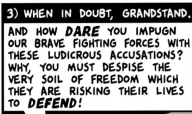

3) WHEN IN DOUBT, GRANDSTAND.

AND HOW *DARE* YOU IMPUGN OUR BRAVE FIGHTING FORCES WITH THESE LUDICROUS ACCUSATIONS? WHY, YOU MUST DESPISE THE VERY SOIL OF FREEDOM WHICH THEY ARE RISKING THEIR LIVES TO *DEFEND!*

ER--NO--THAT'S NOT REALLY--

4) BETTER YET, CHANGE THE SUBJECT ENTIRELY.

FORGET THIS *TORTURE* CRAP! *I* WANT TO KNOW WHY *YOU* HAVEN'T DENOUNCED THE VILE ANTI-AMERICAN COMMENTS OF A GUY WHO WROTE A LETTER TO THE EDITOR IN *NAPERSVILLE, ILLINOIS!*

THE BLOGOSPHERE IS *ABUZZ* WITH *OUTRAGE!*

UH--WHO-- WHAT--?

5) AND OF COURSE, BE UTTERLY SHAMELESS.

YOU LIBERALS JUST WANT TO HURT THE PRESIDENT! THIS IS NOTHING MORE THAN THE POLITICS OF *PERSONAL DESTRUCTION!*

WE CONSERVATIVES ARE FAR TOO *PRINCIPLED* TO EVER BEHAVE IN SUCH A MANNER.

I'M-- I'M SPEECHLESS.

PRECISELY MY INTENTION.

TOM TOMORROW © 2005

127

THIS MODERN WORLD

by TOM TOMORROW

NOTHING TO SEE HERE

MOVE ALONG, MOVE ALONG

WHAT'S THE BIG **DEAL** ABOUT A CONSERVATIVE REPORTER ASKING A FEW QUESTIONS AT WHITE HOUSE PRESS BRIEFINGS?

SCOTT, WHY DO LIBERALS STUBBORN-LY REFUSE TO ACKNOWLEDGE THE PRESIDENT'S SHEER **GREATNESS** AND OBVIOUS **INFALLIBILITY**?

WHY, I'M GLAD YOU ASKED THAT QUESTION, JEFF!

WHO **CARES** IF HE WAS ACTUALLY A PRETEND JOURNALIST WORKING WITHOUT PAY FOR A PARTISAN REPUBLICAN WEBSITE?

JUST BECAUSE SOMEONE DOESN'T HAVE A "JOB" OR ANY "WRITING EXPERIENCE"--

--IT DOESN'T MEAN HE CAN'T BE A BIG-TIME "REPORTER"!

WHAT DOES IT **MATTER** THAT HE APPEARS TO HAVE GAINED REGULAR ACCESS TO THE WHITE HOUSE UNDER AN ASSUMED NAME AND WITHOUT A STANDARD BACK-GROUND CHECK?

THAT SORT OF THING HAPPENS **ALL** THE TIME!

WHITE HOUSE SECURITY PEOPLE ARE **VERY** EASY GOING!

AND SO **WHAT** IF A BACKGROUND CHECK WOULD HAVE REVEALED WHAT LIBERAL BLOGGERS SOON DISCOVERED--THAT HE APPARENTLY HAD A SECRET LIFE AS A TAX-DELINQUENT, PORN-SITE-OPERATING **MALE PROSTITUTE**?

IT'S **OUTRAGEOUS**--THE WAY THESE BLOGGERS VIOLATED HIS **PRIVACY**, I MEAN!

IT'S GETTING SO A MAN CAN'T EVEN POST NAKED PICTURES OF HIMSELF ON THE **INTERNET** ANYMORE!

THERE'S ONLY **ONE EXPLANATION** FOR THE LIBERAL OBSESSION WITH THIS STORY--

--THEY **HATE GAY PEOPLE**! LEFT WING **INTOLERANCE** IS THE ONLY **REAL** SCANDAL HERE!

OTHER THAN THAT--NO SCANDAL WHATSOEVER!

NO, SIREE! NONE AT ALL!

OKAY, THEN.

YEP.

TOM TOMORROW©2005

THIS MODERN WORLD

by TOM TOMORROW

Panel 1:

BOY, THE THREAT OF TERRORISM HAS REALLY CHANGED *EVERYTHING!*

IT SURE *HAS!* I DON'T THINK WE'LL *EVER* LIVE IN A WORLD AS SAFE AS THE ONE *WE* GREW UP IN!

UM--EXCUSE ME--

Panel 2:

IF I'M NOT MISTAKEN, YOU GUYS GREW UP IN A WORLD IN WHICH TWO RIVAL SUPERPOWERS HAD IMMENSE NUCLEAR ARSENALS AIMED AT EACH OTHER, POISED TO LAUNCH AT A *MOMENT'S NOTICE.*

DO YOU *HONESTLY* BELIEVE THAT PEOPLE FELT SAFER *THEN*--WITH THE THREAT OF *GLOBAL ANNHILATION* HANGING OVER THEIR HEADS LIKE THE SWORD OF *DAMOCLES*?

Panel 3:

Panel 4:

BOY, THIS COUNTRY IS MORE POLITICALLY DIVIDED *NOW* THAN *EVER BEFORE* IN *HISTORY!*

IT SURE *IS!* I DON'T THINK THINGS WERE *THIS* BAD DURING THE *CIVIL WAR!*

UM--EXCUSE ME--

OH, NEVER MIND.

TOM TOMORROW©2005

THIS MODERN WORLD

by TOM TOMORROW

Panel 1:

A PROBLEM FOR THE CONSUMER DEBT INDUSTRY: THEY'D **LIKE** TO KEEP HANDING OUT CREDIT CARDS LIKE **HALLOWEEN CANDY**--

GREAT NEWS, ROVER! YOU'RE PRE-APPROVED FOR A **TITANIUM MISTERCARD**!

WOOF!

Panel 2:

--BUT THEY'D PREFER **NOT** TO BE BURDENED BY ANY OF THE ATTENDANT **RISK**!

UH OH! LOOKS LIKE ONE **ROVER Q. DOGG** IS DEFAULTING ON HIS **BALANCE**!

DAMMIT! **HOW** IS THIS INDUSTRY SUPPOSED TO MAINTAIN A $30 BILLION A YEAR PROFIT MARGIN IN THE FACE OF SUCH **IRRESPONSIBLE BEHAVIOR**?

Panel 3:

SO THEY DO WHAT **ANYONE** WOULD DO IN THEIR SITUATION--THEY ASK CONGRESS TO **REWRITE THE LAW**!

YES, SENATOR, THAT'S RIGHT--WE'D LIKE A BANKRUPTCY BILL THAT **REALLY STICKS IT** TO YOUR CONSTITUENTS! A BILL THAT COULDN'T **BE** MORE BIASED IN **OUR FAVOR**!

NO PROBLEMO! WE'LL GET RIGHT TO WORK!

Mis'er Card

Panel 4:

REPUBLICANS (AND A HANDFUL OF DEMOCRATS) GO SO FAR AS TO DISALLOW ANY EXEMPTIONS IN THE BILL FOR MILITARY PERSONNEL, THE INFIRM OR THE **ELDERLY**--

BEGONE, DEADBEAT! YOUR HUMBLE ABODE IS NOW THE PROPERTY OF MY GOOD FRIENDS--AND GENEROUS SUPPORTERS--AT **MISTERCARD**!

BWAH HA HA HA HA HA!

Panel 5:

--WHILE LEAVING IN PLACE AN ENORMOUS "ASSET PROTECTION" LOOPHOLE FOR THE **WEALTHY**!*

SO I'M HAVING A LITTLE **CASH FLOW** PROBLEM! AM I SUPPOSED TO GO LIVE IN A **HOMELESS SHELTER** OR SOMETHING?

PERISH THE THOUGHT, GOOD SIR!

* FORCING RELUCTANT CARTOONISTS TO RESORT TO THE OLD "SILENT MOVIE VILLAIN" CLICHÉ...

Panel 6:

IT REALLY MAKES YOU WONDER IF THERE'S **ANYTHING** REPUBLICANS CAN DO THAT WOULD ALIENATE THEIR RANK-AND-FILE...

HONEY, WHY IS SENATOR WHIPLASH TYING YOUR MOTHER TO THE **RAILROAD TRACKS**?

I DON'T KNOW, DEAR--BUT I'M **SURE** HE HAS HER BEST INTERESTS AT HEART!

BWAH HA HA HA HA!

TOM TOMORROW©2005

THIS MODERN WORLD

by TOM TOMORROW

WELCOME TO THE OFFICIAL *BUSH NEWS NETWORK!* I'M *KAREN RYAN!*

OUR TOP STORY TONIGHT: IRAQI DETAINEES ARE TREATED *VERY, VERY WELL!* SPECIAL CORRESPONDENT *ARMSTRONG WILLIAMS* HAS THIS *EXCLUSIVE REPORT!*

THANKS, KAREN! I'M HERE IN A PENTHOUSE SUITE AT THE PLUSH *BAGHDAD RITZ* WITH A *TYPICAL IRAQI DETAINEE*--WHO SAYS HE HASN'T BEEN MISTREATED AT *ALL!*

FAR FROM IT! THE ROOM SERVICE IS *EXCELLENT*-- AND I *LOVE* THE FLUFFY PILLOWS!

THANKS, ARMSTRONG! MOVING TO DOMESTIC NEWS--OUR *JEFF GANNON* WENT MANO-A-MANO WITH NEW D.N.C. CHAIR *HOWARD DEAN* EARLIER TODAY!

WHAT'S THAT, GOVERNOR DEAN? YOU SAY DEMOCRATS ARE COMPLETELY DIVORCED FROM *REALITY*? AND YOU *HATE AMERICA*?

I *SEE!*

VERY *ENLIGHTENING*, JEFF! IN A RELATED STORY--DESPITE THE OPPOSITION OF A FEW OBSTRUCTIONIST *DEMOCRATS*, THE OVERWHELMING MAJORITY OF AMERICANS *SUPPORT* THE PRESIDENT'S PLAN TO *SAVE SOCIAL SECURITY!*

ARMSTRONG WILLIAMS HAS MORE, IN THIS REPORT THAT HE, UH, TAPED BEFORE HE WENT TO BAGHDAD.

OR AFTER HE GOT BACK.

OR SOMETHING.

THANKS, KAREN! I'M HERE WITH A *TYPICAL YOUNG AMERICAN* WHO SAYS HE IS *VERY CONCERNED* ABOUT THE FUTURE OF SOCIAL SECURITY!

I SURE *AM!* AND THAT'S WHY *I* WANT MY OWN *PRIVATE ACCOUNT!*

AHEM! PSST-- PSSST-- *PSST!*

SORRY! PERSONAL ACCOUNT!

THERE YOU HAVE IT! COMING UP NEXT--*JEFF GANNON* AND *ARMSTRONG WILLIAMS* EXPLAIN WHY YOU *JUST CAN'T TRUST* THE *MAINSTREAM MEDIA!*

ALSO, WE INVESTIGATE: IS GEORGE BUSH THE WISEST LEADER *EVER?*

FIRST THESE MESSAGES!

THIS MODERN WORLD

by TOM TOMORROW

IT BEGINS WITH A STARTLING REVELATION.

CNN HAS OBTAINED VIDEO FOOTAGE AND SUBSTANTIATING DOCUMENTS WHICH PROVE BEYOND ANY DOUBT THAT SECRETARY OF STATE *CONDOLEEZA RICE*--

--IS *ACTUALLY* A HIDEOUS MULTI-TENTACLED ALIEN BEING WHICH FEEDS ON A STEADY DIET OF *HUMAN BRAINS!*

MORE *BRAINS,* PLEASE!

WE JUST GOT A FRESH SHIPMENT IN FROM GITMO, MADAME SECRETARY!

THE RIGHT-WING OBFUSCATION MACHINE QUICKLY SPRINGS INTO ACTION!

SECRETARY RICE'S DIETARY PREFERENCES ARE HER *OWN BUSINESS*--AND I FIND THIS INVASION OF HER PRIVACY *DEPLORABLE!*

THE ISSUE ISN'T *BRAIN EATING*--THE ISSUE IS *LIBERAL XENOPHOBIA!*

AND WHILE LIBERALS DEBATE THE APPROPRIATE COURSE OF ACTION--

I THINK IT WOULD BE BEST TO POLITELY OVERLOOK THE MATTER-- LEST WE FIND OURSELVES SWEPT UP IN THE POLITICS OF *PERSONAL DESTRUCTION!*

THAT *WOULD* BE DISAGREEABLE!

--*CONSERVATIVES* STAY ON THE *ATTACK!*

THE PURPORTED MEMO FROM SECRETARY RICE DEMANDING THAT BRAINS BE HARVESTED MORE "EFFICIENTLY" IS PRINTED ON A STRANGE, OTHERWORLDLY *METALLIC* SUBSTANCE--

--BUT EVERYONE *KNOWS* THAT *REAL* WHITE HOUSE MEMOS ARE ALWAYS PRINTED ON *PAPER!*

IT IS AN *OBVIOUS FORGERY!*

AND AFTER WOLF BLITZER RESIGNS IN DISGRACE, THE WHOLE THING IS QUIETLY FORGOTTEN.

HEY, WASN'T CONDI SUPPOSED TO BE SOME KIND OF SPACE MONSTER OR SOMETHING?

NAH, DIDN'T YOU HEAR? THAT WAS ALL A BIG FRAUD! THE MEMO WAS A *FAKE!*

OH! WELL, *THAT'S* CERTAINLY A RELIEF!

Tom Tomorrow©2005

132

THIS MODERN WORLD

by TOM TOMORROW

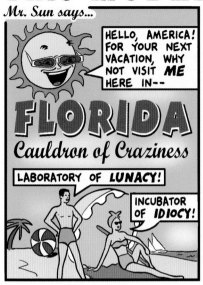

Mr. Sun says...

HELLO, AMERICA! FOR YOUR NEXT VACATION, WHY NOT VISIT **ME** HERE IN--

FLORIDA
Cauldron of Craziness

LABORATORY OF **LUNACY!**

INCUBATOR OF **IDIOCY!**

THAT'S RIGHT--**FLORIDA!** NOT ONLY WILL YOU FROLIC IN THE **SURF** AND **SUNSHINE**--

--YOU'LL ALSO WITNESS FIRSTHAND THE NATION'S FOREMOST BREEDING GROUND OF SHEER POLITICAL **DERANGEMENT!**

WHO COULD **EVER** FORGET THE CHAOS OF THE 2000 ELECTION? HANGING CHADS, PURGED VOTER LISTS, G.O.P. STAFFERS STAGING FAKE RIOTS--AND A RECOUNT OVERSEEN BY **KATHERINE HARRIS** AND **JEB BUSH?**

CALIFORNIA'S GOT **NOTHING** ON **US!**

MORE RECENTLY, OF COURSE, OUR GOVERNOR SIDED WITH FUNDAMENTALIST WACKOS IN THE **SCHIAVO** CASE--

--UNLEASHING A NATIONAL **ORGY** OF POLITICAL GRANDSTANDING AND EXPLOITATION!

MATCH **THAT,** NEVADA!

WHY **DOES** FLORIDA SPAWN SO MUCH FATUITY? IS IT SOMETHING IN THE **DRINKING WATER?** AN ANCIENT SEMINOLE **CURSE?**

WHATEVER IT IS--FOR GOD'S SAKE, STAY **AWAY!** SAVE YOURSELVES BEFORE IT'S TOO LATE--**MMMPH!**

AHEM! WHAT BIFF **MEANT** TO SAY IS, COME EXPERIENCE THE **MYSTERY** OF FLORIDA FOR **YOURSELF!**

WHY IF YOU HURRY ON DOWN, YOU CAN WATCH THE FLORIDA STATE LEGISLATURE DEBATE A BILL TO STAMP OUT **"LEFTIST TOTALITARIANISM"** BY **"DICTATOR PROFESSORS!"**

SOUNDS **UTTERLY INSANE,** DOESN'T IT?

IN OTHER WORDS, IT'S JUST **BUSINESS AS USUAL**--

--IN **FLORIDA!!**

TOM TOMORROW ©2005

133

THIS MODERN WORLD

by TOM TOMORROW

IT'S **APPALLING** THAT THE LEFT SUPPORTED THE REMOVAL OF TERRI'S **FEEDING TUBE**! I JUST DON'T UNDERSTAND WHY YOU LIBERALS HATE **LIFE** SO MUCH!

ER, YES, WELL--YOUR NEWFOUND REVERENCE FOR THE SANCTITY OF LIFE IN ALL ITS MYRIAD FORMS IS CERTAINLY **TOUCHING**...

...BUT, IF YOU'LL FORGIVE ME FOR BRINGING UP THE OBVIOUS, I CAN'T HELP BUT WONDER IF IT EXTENDS TO THE UNTOLD TENS OF THOUSANDS OF IRAQI CIVILIANS--POSSIBLE AS MANY AS ONE **HUNDRED** THOUSAND--KILLED AS A RESULT OF GEORGE BUSH'S LITTLE **WAR**...

...MOST OF WHOM PRESUMABLY HAD ACTUAL **LIVES**, NOT TO MENTION FUNCTIONING **BRAINS**...

IT'S **APPALLING** THAT THE LEFT WOULD TRY TO POLITICIZE A LITTLE **COLLATERAL DAMAGE**! I JUST DON'T UNDERSTAND WHY YOU LIBERALS HATE **FREEDOM** SO MUCH!

AND ROUND AND ROUND WE GO.

TOM TOMORROW©2005

by TOM TOMORROW

IT'S TIME FOR ANOTHER LOOK AT THE SECRETIVE AND DUPLICITOUS WORLD OF--

THE VAST LEFT WING CONSPIRACY

THEY DEVIOUSLY *PUBLISH* THEIR OPINIONS IN BOOKS AND PERIODICALS WHICH ARE DISTRIBUTED THROUGH A SHADOWY NETWORK OF "*BOOKSTORES*" AND "*NEWSSTANDS!*"

LOOK WHAT *I* FOUND HIDDEN UNDER JUNIOR'S *MATTRESS!*

PAUL *KRUGMAN?* WHERE DID YOU GET *THAT* FILTH?!

PAUL KRUGMAN — THE GREAT UNRAVE...

AND THEY INSIDIOUSLY MAKE *MOVIES* WHICH ARE COVERTLY SHOWN IN *MEGAPLEXES* ACROSS THE *COUNTRY!*

TWO TICKETS FOR "FAHRENHEIT 911," COMRADE!

DEATH TO CAPITALISM! FOURTEEN DOLLARS, PLEASE.

7:3... Peggy

THOSE WHO KNOW THE PROPER *FREQUENCY* CAN LISTEN TO THEIR CLANDESTINE *RADIO* BROADCASTS!

--THIS IS *SAM SEDER* ON *AIR AMERICA RADIO!*

FOR GOD'S SAKE-- TURN DOWN THE VOLUME BEFORE SOMEONE *REPORTS* US!

AND ON THE *INTERNET*, THEY USE *SECRET CODE NAMES* TO PUBLICLY ADVOCATE THE OVERTHROW OF THE CURRENT *GOVERNMENT!*

"ATRIOS" IS URGING PEOPLE TO VOTE FOR *DEMOCRATS* IN 2006-- AND "KOS" *CONCURS!*

DOES THEIR TREACHERY KNOW NO *BOUNDS?*

SO BE *WARNED*, AMERICA! THESE CONNIVING LEFTISTS ARE *EVERYWHERE*--SCHEMING TO SWAY PUBLIC OPINION WITH THEIR *DEVIOUS, UNDERHANDED TACTICS!*

IF REPUBLICANS DIDN'T CONTROL ALL THREE BRANCHES OF GOVERNMENT AND A BROAD SWATH OF THE MAINSTREAM MEDIA--

--WE WOULDN'T STAND A *CHANCE*--AGAINST THE *VAST LEFT WING CONSPIRACY!!*

TOM TOMORROW ©2005

THIS MODERN WORLD

by TOM TOMORROW

THE WACKY MISADVENTURES OF THE OVER-ZEALOUS REPUBLICAN STAFFER!

IN 2001, HE WORKED AS A CIA ANALYST.

DIRECTOR TENET, AS FAR AS I'M CONCERNED, THE CASE FOR WMD'S IS A *SLAM DUNK!*

THANKS, OVERZEALOUS STAFFER! I'LL LET THE PRESIDENT *KNOW!*

AFTER THAT, HE DID SOME VOLUNTEER WORK FOR THE BUSH CAMPAIGN--

HERE'S A LIST OF CITIZENS WHO SHOULD *NOT* BE ADMITTED TO THE PRESIDENT'S PUBLIC RALLY!

IF ANYONE ASKS, JUST TELL THEM THAT *I* GAVE IT TO YOU!

--BEFORE JOINING THE DEPARTMENT OF EDUCATION.

I'VE GOT A *GREAT IDEA*, SECRETARY PAIGE! LET'S PAY A COLUMNIST $240,000 TO PROMOTE NO CHILD LEFT BEHIND!

DO WHAT YOU WANT, OVERZEALOUS STAFFER! WE'RE ALL *FAR* TOO BUSY TO SUPERVISE YOU!

THAT WAS FOLLOWED BY A BRIEF STINT IN THE WHITE HOUSE PRESS OFFICE--

TRUST ME, SCOTT--JEFF GANNON DOESN'T NEED A *BACKGROUND CHECK!* I'LL JUST KEEP GIVING HIM *DAY PASSES!*

SURE, O.Z., WHATEVER YOU SAY.

--AND AN EVEN BRIEFER STINT AS AN ADVISOR TO TOM DELAY.

SO YOU REALLY DON'T THINK ANYONE WILL CARE IF I ACCEPT ALL THESE LAVISH GIFTS FROM LOBBYISTS?

NAH--WHY *WOULD* THEY?

MOST RECENTLY, HE WAS SEEN WORKING WITH SENATOR MEL MARTINEZ.

HERE'S A MEMO ABOUT THE POLITICAL RAMIFICATIONS OF THE SCHIAVO CASE, SENATOR!

UH--GREAT, THANKS. I'LL LOOK AT IT AFTER MY MEETING WITH TOM HARKIN.

WE DON'T KNOW WHERE HE'LL TURN UP NEXT, BUT ONE THING'S FOR SURE--

THE DETAINEE IS READY FOR INTERROGATION, O.Z!

THANK YOU, PRIVATE! I'LL TAKE IT FROM HERE!

--ZANY HIJINKS ARE *CERTAIN* TO FOLLOW!

TOM TOMORROW © 2005

THIS MODERN WORLD
by TOM TOMORROW

REPUBLICANS BELIEVE THE DARNDEST THINGS

AN OCCASIONAL LOOK AT THE WORLD AS CONSERVATIVES SEE IT

---

1. PAT ROBERTSON AND JAMES DOBSON REALLY DON'T HAVE MUCH INFLUENCE OVER THE G.O.P.

YOU SAY THEY HAVE LARGE FOLLOWINGS AND AN AGGRESSIVELY CONSERVATIVE AGENDA?

I'LL BE DARNED! CAN'T SAY I'VE HEARD OF THEM!

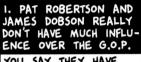

---

2. AN OBSCURE COLLEGE PROFESSOR NAMED WARD CHURCHILL HAS **UNPRECEDENTED** INFLUENCE OVER DEMOCRATS.

WHEN WARD SAYS TO DENOUNCE SOMEONE, MY ONLY QUESTION IS **HOW VITRIOLICALLY?**

I'D BE **LOST** WITHOUT HIS CONSTANT COUNSEL!

---

3. YOU CAN'T TRUST **ANYTHING** YOU READ IN THE MAINSTREAM MEDIA.

THE WEATHER FORECAST CALLS FOR RAIN TODAY.

YEAH, THE LIBERALS WOULD **LIKE** US TO BELIEVE THAT, WOULDN'T THEY?

---

4. CONSERVATIVE BLOGGERS SHOULD BE GIVEN **EVERY** BENEFIT OF THE DOUBT.

"THE RAVING BLABBERMOUTH" SAYS THAT IT WILL NEVER, EVER RAIN AGAIN **ANYWHERE!**

WHY DOESN'T THE M.S.M. REPORT **THAT?**

---

5. PHARMACISTS HAVE THE RIGHT TO WITHHOLD PRESCRIPTIONS AT THEIR OWN DISCRETION.

VIAGRA? NO PROBLEM.

BIRTH CONTROL? GET LOST, SLUT.

---

6. JUDGES ARE FAIR GAME.

YES--THE MOST **DANGEROUS** GAME!

YOU'VE GOT **TEN MINUTES,** JUSTICE KENNEDY-- THEN FRIST AND I ARE COMING **AFTER** YOU!

---

7. MICHAEL MOORE AND ANN COULTER ARE TWO SIDES OF THE SAME COIN.

THE IRAQ WAR WAS BASED ON LIES.

WOULDN'T IT BE **HILARIOUS** IF A TERRORIST MURDERED ALL THE REPORTERS AND EDITORS AT THE NEW YORK TIMES? HAW, HAW, HAW!

SEE? EXACTLY THE **SAME!**

TOM TOMORROW©2005

THIS MODERN WORLD

by TOM TOMORROW

THE EXCITING ADVENTURES OF

SPARKMAN

AND THE BLINKSTER

THIS ISSUE: TRUTH OR **CONSEQUENCES!**

ON A ROUTINE PATROL, OUR HEROES OVERHEAR A **DISTURBING CON-VERSATION...**

IT'S **LUDICROUS** FOR AMNESTY INTERNATIONAL TO COMPARE GUANTANAMO TO A **GULAG!**

YES--THE GULAGS WERE **FORCED LABOR CAMPS!** PRISONERS AT GITMO SIT IN **CAGES** ALL DAY!

AND IT'S **IDIOTIC** OF THESE LIBERAL COLUMNISTS TO CLAIM THAT **ONE HUNDRED DETAINEES** HAVE BEEN KILLED BY U.S. INTERROGATORS!

YES--THE **ARMY** SAYS THE NUMBER IS LESS THAN **THIRTY!**

AHEM.

ARE YOU GENTLEMEN SUGGESTING THAT THE ABUSES OF ABU GHRAIB AND BAGRAM CAN BE **EXCUSED--**

--BECAUSE THE UNITED STATES OF AMERICA IS **NOT AS BAD** AS RUSSIA UNDER **STALIN--**

--AND **FEWER** DETAINEES HAVE BEEN **TORTURED TO DEATH** THAN SOME CRITICS HAVE **CLAIMED?!**

YES, THAT'S RIGHT!

GOD BLESS AMERICA!

SIGH...I'M AFRAID THIS CALLS FOR DRASTIC MEASURES, BLINKSTER--

NO--YOU DON'T MEAN--

YES--

--THE **HEAVY-HANDED RAY OF IRONIC JUSTICE!!**

BZZRRAAAP

THEY'RE **GONE**, SPARKMAN! WHERE DID THE RAY **SEND** THEM?

TO **IRAQ**, BLINKSTER--WHERE THEY'RE ABOUT TO BE PICKED UP AS **SUSPECTED INSURGENTS!**

GOODNESS-- THAT **IS** IRONIC!

INDEED IT IS, CHUM-- **AND** HEAVY-HANDED!

ALL IN A DAY'S WORK--FOR **SPARKMAN** AND THE **BLINKSTER!**

TOM TOMORROW©2005

THIS MODERN WORLD

by TOM TOMORROW

SUPPORTING THE TROOPS

FEATURING

THE 18 TO 22-YEAR-OLD REPUBLICAN THINK TANK INTERNS

THE ARMY IS HAVING TROUBLE RECRUITING 18 TO 22-YEAR-OLDS-- AND THE TROOPS ARE STRETCHED TO THE *BREAKING POINT* AS A RESULT!

IF ONLY THERE WERE SOME WAY *WE* COULD HELP!

HMMM...

MAYBE WE COULD ADVISE THE ARMY ON THE BEST WAYS TO *REACH* THE 18 TO 22-YEAR-OLD MARKET-- FOR A SMALL *CONSULTING FEE,* OF COURSE!

A PERSON'S GOTTA MAKE A LIVING!

OR MAYBE WE COULD FORM AN INNER-CITY *OUTREACH PROGRAM*--TO CONVINCE MORE 18 TO 22-YEAR-OLD *POOR PEOPLE* TO ENLIST!

WE COULD EXPLAIN TO THEM ABOUT *PATRIOTISM* AND STUFF!

THEN AGAIN, MAYBE WE'RE *ALREADY* DOING ALL WE *CAN* FOR THE TROOPS--BY FOCUSING ON OUR *OWN CAREERS!*

YEAH! WE'RE FIGHTING THE WAR AT *HOME!*

THE TROOPS *NEED* US HERE!

WELL, I'D BETTER GET BACK TO WORK--I'VE GOT TO FINISH A SET OF TALKING POINTS EXTOLLING THE VIRTUES OF A LEAN AND MEAN *ALL-VOLUNTEER ARMY!*

I'M STUDYING THE FEASIBILITY OF SIMULTANEOUS INVASIONS OF IRAN AND SYRIA-- USING *EXISTING TROOP LEVELS!*

IT'S A TOUGH JOB--BUT *SOME* 18 TO 22-YEAR-OLD HAS TO DO IT!

TOM TOMORROW ©2005

THIS MODERN WORLD

by TOM TOMORROW

The Very Bad Idea

by Tom Tomorrow

ONCE UPON A TIME, THE LEADER OF A GREAT BIG NATION HAD A VERY BAD IDEA.

AND WE MUST **PURSUE** MY VERY BAD IDEA **IMMEDIATELY!** THE FUTURE OF OUR NATION **DEPENDS** ON IT!

HURRAY FOR OUR NATION!

HURRAY FOR THE VERY BAD IDEA!

SOME PEOPLE TRIED TO POINT OUT WHAT A VERY BAD IDEA IT **WAS**...

IT IS CERTAINLY NOT A **GOOD** IDEA--

--BUT RATHER, BY DEFINITION, A VERY **BAD** IDEA!

...BUT NO ONE LISTENED TO **THEM**.

AT FIRST, THE VERY BAD IDEA APPEARED TO BE WORKING OUT WELL.

I GUESS THIS PROVES THAT **OPPONENTS** OF THE VERY BAD IDEA WERE AS **WRONG** AS WRONG CAN **BE!**

HEH! WHAT FUN WE SHALL HAVE, GLOATING EXCESSIVELY AT THEIR EXPENSE!

VERY BAD IDEA ACCOMPLISHED

BUT EVENTUALLY, MORE AND MORE PEOPLE BEGAN TO SUSPECT THAT IT HAD BEEN A **VERY** BAD IDEA INDEED.

IF ONLY THERE WERE SOME WAY WE COULD HAVE **KNOWN!**

HOW COULD WE HAVE **POSSIBLY** FORESEEN SUCH AN OUTCOME?

VERY BAD IDEA NOT WORKING OUT SO WELL AFTER ALL

FORTUNATELY, THE LEADER OF THE BIG NATION WAS **UNDETERRED!**

WE MUST **CONTINUE** TO PURSUE THE VERY BAD IDEA--OR ELSE OUR PURSUIT OF THE BAD IDEA SO FAR WILL HAVE BEEN IN **VAIN!**

YOU CAN'T ARGUE WITH LOGIC LIKE **THAT!**

AND IF YOU **DO**-- WE WON'T **LISTEN!**

AND THEY ALL LIVED HAPPILY EVER AFTER, EXCEPT FOR THE ONES WHO DIDN'T.

TOM TOMORROW©2005... www.thismodernworld.com

140

THIS MODERN WORLD

by TOM TOMORROW

THE MINUTE SHE WALKED IN THE DOOR I KNEW SHE WAS TROUBLE.

YOU'VE GOT TO HELP ME, MISTER PENGUIN! SOMEONE HAS STOLEN MY *IDENTITY!*

Sparky T. Penguin

Private Investigator

LOT OF THAT GOING AROUND.

SHE TOLD ME HER STORY. A REAL TEARJERKER.

A FEW YEARS BACK I MANAGED TO GET SOME MONEY TUCKED AWAY--BUT SOMEONE HAS DRAINED MY ACCOUNTS AND RUN UP *BILLIONS* OF DOLLARS OF DEBT IN MY NAME!

AND NOT ONLY THAT-- PEOPLE ARE ACCUSING ME OF THE MOST *OUTLANDISH* THINGS! TORTURE, KIDNAPPING, UNJUSTIFIED *WARS!* I DON'T KNOW HOW I'M *EVER* GOING TO RESTORE MY REPU- TATION!

BUT I KNEW WHO SHE WAS--AND I WASN'T BUYING THE INNOCENT ACT.

SORRY, SISTER. WE BOTH KNOW WHO DID ALL THOSE THINGS IN YOUR NAME--YOUR BOYFRIEND *GEORGE*, THE *MOB BOSS.* WORD ON THE STREET IS, YOU HAD A CHANCE TO KICK HIM OUT LAST *NOVEM- BER*--BUT YOU DECIDED THAT YOU *LIKED HIS STYLE!*

SOB--IT'S *TRUE*--

--HALF OF ME WANTED TO *DUMP* HIM--BUT SLIGHTLY MORE THAN HALF OF ME WANTED HIM TO *STAY*...

OH, MISTER PENGUIN--HAVE I MADE A *TERRIBLE MISTAKE?*

YEAH, SWEETHEART, YOU HAVE... AND YOU'RE GONNA HAVE TO *LIVE* WITH IT...

THE HELL OF IT IS-- SO ARE THE *REST* OF US...

I WAS JUST A TWO-BIT SHAMUS IN A SEEDY OFFICE ON THE WRONG SIDE OF TOWN...THAT DAME HAD BIG- GER PROBLEMS THAN *I* KNEW HOW TO SOLVE...

TOM TOMORROW © 2005

ALSO BY TOM TOMORROW

GREETINGS FROM THIS MODERN WORLD

TUNE IN TOMORROW

THE WRATH OF SPARKY

WHEN PENGUINS ATTACK!

PENGUIN SOUP FOR THE SOUL

THE GREAT BIG BOOK OF TOMORROW

AND THE INEVITABLE WEBSITE

WWW.THISMODERNWORLD.COM